PRAISE FOR *IDEAS, INFLUENCE, AND INCOME*

"Tanya Hall and her team insisted that I develop an idea and monetize it with a book as one component . . . and that is the best publishing advice I have ever received. Now, she has written the story behind that advice in *Ideas, Influence, and Income*. If you want to capture ideas and leverage your influence to build a sustainable business, then Tanya Hall can show you how!"

—**BARRY BANTHER,** author of *A Leader's Gift*

"Tanya Hall and Greenleaf have pioneered the next-generation publishing model, treating authors as true partners and cocreating extraordinary work. Tanya offers practical wisdom, grounded in extensive experience, to convert your ideas into instruments of great influence, contribution, and wealth. My own success is a testament to the power of this wisdom."

—**SHIRZAD CHAMINE,** *New York Times* best-selling
author of *Positive Intelligence*

"Tanya has collected all of her vast experience and hard-earned wisdom in this precious new book. She shines a bright path not just for new writers but for all authors on how best to present their *ideas*, create sustainable *influence*, and maximize *income* with actionable and achievable steps. Her insights and insider knowledge make this book a must read for anyone considering a writing career."

—**JOHN WILLIG,** president of Literary Services, Inc.

"*Ideas, Influence, and Income* is the ultimate guide to writing, publishing, and marketing your book—a cornucopia of wisdom that will help propel you to success. Whether you are planning to write a book or are already a published author, you will benefit greatly from Tanya's approach and knowledge of a highly competitive industry. *Ideas, Influence, and Income* belongs on every writer's bookshelf."

—**JANE WESMAN,** president of Jane Wesman Public Relations,
Inc. and author of *Dive Right In: The Sharks Won't Bite*

"So often people ask me, 'How do I get my ideas published? What's right for my business goals?' At last, I have an answer: Read *Ideas, Influence, and Income*. This smart resource book nails it!"

—**MARY LOU QUINLAN,** *New York Times* best-selling author of *The God Box*

"When authors ask me the best way to publish, I always say, 'You need to talk to Tanya Hall!' Now, with *Ideas, Influence, and Income*, Tanya expertly guides readers through today's confusing publishing world to confidently plan, write, and publish a successful book."

—**SANDY SMITH,** president of Smith Publicity

"I have known Tanya Hall for over a decade and regard her as one of the smartest, most engaging women in the business. After reading her book I'm even more impressed that she invested the time to share her knowledge with the public. She has written the ultimate guide for every aspiring author. She's a brilliant publisher who has witnessed the value of the book as a marketing tool, and she has generously created the road map for crafting a successful publication. As a book packager and publisher, I am incredibly impressed with the detail she provides in *Ideas, Influence, and Income*, and I don't believe there is another book that covers this subject so well. Congratulations Tanya! I'm saving a space on my bookshelf for this one!"

—**JILL COHEN,** founder of Jill Cohen Associates

"So many people have a secret (or not-so-secret) desire to be a published author. Tanya packed this book with practical tips and insights to help would-be authors sharpen their point of view, build an audience, and get their books into readers' hands."

—**MELISSA JOULWAN,** author of the best-selling *Well Fed* cookbook series

"Through her deep experience leading one of the trailblazing companies in the new publishing marketplace, Tanya Hall has had a front-row seat to the transformation and democratization of what had long been a closed, hidebound industry. With this book, she is sharing a wealth of valuable insights she has gained along the way that will particularly benefit the growing universe of thought leaders who care as much, if not more, about moving minds as moving units. It's a smart, practical, and reliable road map for authors who know *where* they want to go but are not sure how to get there."

—**DAN GERSTEIN,** president of Gotham Ghostwriters

"If you are or want to be a nonfiction author and intend to use your book to support a bigger brand and create additional streams of revenue, then read this book immediately. You'd be hard-pressed to find a person more qualified to guide you through the process than Tanya Hall."

—**MICHAEL PORT,** *New York Times* and *Wall Street Journal*
best-selling author of six books, including *Steal the Show*

TANYA HALL

IDEAS, INFLUENCE, AND INCOME

WRITE A BOOK, BUILD YOUR BRAND,
AND LEAD YOUR INDUSTRY

GREENLEAF
BOOK GROUP PRESS

Published by Greenleaf Book Group Press
Austin, Texas
www.gbgpress.com

Distributed by Greenleaf Book Group

For ordering information or special discounts for bulk purchases, please
contact Greenleaf Book Group at PO Box 91869, Austin, TX 78709,
512.891.6100.

Design and composition by Greenleaf Book Group
Cover design by Greenleaf Book Group

Publisher's Cataloging-in-Publication data is available.

Print ISBN: 978-1-62634-514-0

eBook ISBN: 978-1-62634-515-7

Part of the Tree Neutral® program, which offsets the number of trees
consumed in the production and printing of this book by taking proactive
steps, such as planting trees in direct proportion to the number of trees
used: www.treeneutral.com

Printed in the United States of America on acid-free paper

18 19 20 21 22 23   10 9 8 7 6 5 4 3 2 1

First Edition

for Maizy and Sydney
Smart wins

CONTENTS

INTRODUCTION

SOME PEOPLE NEVER TRAVEL WITHOUT EARBUDS in the interest of not having to engage in conversation with the strangers next to them on an airplane. Not me. If my seatmate is willing, I love meeting new people and learning about their lives. In the worst scenario, it's a forced conversation that will end in a matter of hours. That's rarely the case, though, because I have a secret weapon in my icebreaker arsenal.

When I tell my neighbor that I run a publishing company, their face lights up and the conversation goes one of three ways: the person tells me about a book they have recently read that they loved, the person tells me about someone they know who wrote a book, or the person takes a deep breath and tells me about their own book.

People who tell me about their own books are often sheepish. "I think I wrote a good book, but I guess it didn't sell very well," they'll say, or they'll write its lack of success off (so to speak) as a failure by their publicist or publisher, who are usually thrown under the bus in that order.

As we work through the background and diagnose their experience through conversation, I always find myself wishing that I could have met this person before they wrote their book to help them think strategically about its success. Writing a book is a big enough challenge on its own, and often writers are so concerned with finishing the manuscript that they fail to consider the many remaining moving parts of what is essentially a media product launch.

There's a decent chance that I'll never sit next to you on a plane, so my hope is that you will read and use this book as a resource to write and launch your book and to then use it as a springboard for additional brand power and revenue streams.

THE APPROACH

There's a simple framework I use to help authors get the most out of publishing a book. The pillars of that framework are the three themes that make up the title of this book: *Ideas, Influence, and Income.*

Ideas refers to the knowledge or vision you want to share through your content. *Influence* deals with building and impacting your audience. *Income* teaches you how to launch your book and monetize the idea behind it in additional formats to maximize returns.

Each of these areas requires a fair amount of attention to ensure its success. They work together like an ecosystem—if any element is weak, the entire organism suffers. That's why it was important for me to write a book that goes beyond how to publish your manuscript. I also want you to learn how to successfully launch your book and get the most out of the hard work that you put into completing it.

Unless you've been doing this kind of work for over a decade, like yours truly, the knowledge and skills needed to build each of these areas are rarely found in one person. For that reason, throughout this book, I encourage you to seek help when you get stuck, no matter where you get stuck. Losing momentum can land your big idea in a coma, and that makes for a boring airplane story.

WHY WRITE A BOOK?

We live in the information age, and with that comes information overload.

People are inundated with sales calls, spam mail, and other unwelcome marketing materials cluttering their mailboxes, email accounts, and televisions.

People are tuning out. Direct mail ends up in the trash, emails are deleted without being opened, and buying radio or television airtime is too expensive unless you've got big business dollars.

So how can an expert or visionary break through the clutter, spread an idea, and connect with an audience? The answer: Write a book.

Have you ever attempted to declutter your home, only to scratch your head about what to do with your (physical) books? Books have a certain sanctity, a high perceived value that makes people hesitate to discard them. It's as if they have a life of their own. This value conveys to their authors. Becoming an author sets you apart as an expert on a higher level, someone who has stepped forward to move from tribesman to elder.

Writing a book also helps you to better understand how to serve your audience. In the *Ideas* section, you'll learn how to use the writing process to get a clear picture of the audience you serve and how to use their feedback to refine the angle you take on presenting your message. Again, a book launch is a product launch, and it deserves some research and development time to lock in the right messaging.

And of course, a book builds the backbone of our *Influence* and *Income* efforts. Along with the increased visibility and credibility that come from a strong book launch, the content you develop while writing your book can be repurposed into countless tools and new products to support your big idea.

IS THIS BOOK RIGHT FOR YOU?

The framework behind this book is specifically designed to support non-fiction authors intending to use their own book to support a bigger brand effort. That said, fiction authors will find that much of this guidance also applies to their work, especially in the *Ideas* and *Influence* sections.

The concepts outlined in this book also apply to authors who have already written a book but aren't sure how to launch it—and even those who have launched with lackluster results and are looking for a resource to breathe new life into their book's performance. While there's no silver bullet formula for quick book sales here, you'll surely learn something that will help you get more out of your work.

Whether you read this book from cover to cover or choose to focus on the section(s) that best equips you to develop, promote, or monetize your content, I'll continue to remind you to enlist help if it feels overwhelming. I repeat this simply because I've seen so many authors try to do too much, too quickly by themselves and burn out before the book has a chance to reach its full potential. Be patient, be strategic, and be smart about developing a plan for the entire lifecycle of your book. I will give you all of the tools to do so in the following pages.

IN GRATITUDE

I often tell my authors to think about what they are asking of their audience when they're trying to sell books. It's not about convincing someone to spend twenty dollars on your book. Twenty dollars is not a huge sum of money. It's about convincing them to give you two weeks, or however long it takes that person to finish a book, of their time and interest. An author's biggest fight is for mindshare.

Being especially attuned to that idea, this book is built to give you a roadmap for writing, publishing, launching, and monetizing your book idea. It may take you more than two weeks to read, and it will certainly take longer to implement these ideas. My mother used to say that "the easy thing is rarely the right thing," and that feels appropriate here.

To the extent that *Ideas, Influence, and Income* helps you to successfully bring your idea to the world, I am grateful to contribute. I hope to one day sit beside you on an airplane and enjoy a champagne toast to your success.

PART 1

IDEAS

Chapter 1

THE IMPORTANCE OF OWNING YOUR IDEA

No army can withstand the strength
of an idea whose time has come.
—Victor Hugo

ALL BOOKS START OUT AS AN IDEA—a concept or thought that grows and builds into something bigger. *I want to help people save for retirement. I want to teach people to be healthy. I want to spread the word about a social cause.*

Whatever the idea is, it has the potential in the moment of its creation to become action. It is a vision for the future—for a better future, in most cases—that does not yet exist in a tangible form. The word *idea* suggests an opportunity to make that better or new future a reality. And the next step in seizing that opportunity is to determine how to make it real.

Should you start a company based on the idea? Record a podcast? Host events? Start a blog? Raise money? Write news articles? Write a book?

Quickly, your idea has developed a bit of momentum, which means you'll need to think strategically about how to get the most out of it moving forward.

For many authors, a book plays a key role in getting their big idea out into the world. Publishing a book isn't always the final goal, but it's often one of many pieces in a marketing strategy that establishes them as experts and helps them reach more people.

A perfect example of this is Joe Cross, an expert in the world of juice diets. On the verge of turning forty years old, he was a hundred pounds overweight. When he tried to imagine his life twenty years into the future, he didn't like what he saw.

His idea: "To reboot my life and go back to plants."

When that idea paid off for Joe via a major health turnaround thanks to juicing, he decided to share his story with more people, beginning with his successful documentary, *Fat, Sick, and Nearly Dead*. He then developed his idea further by adding a coaching business, an online support group, juice recipes, and, of course, books.

Joe had a vision to capitalize on the success of the documentary by releasing four books in two years. Under traditional publishing guidelines, this timeline objective was highly unlikely to pan out. Between shopping for an agent, finding the right publisher, and producing the content, the first of the books would launch well after the documentary's buzz died down. On top of that, he'd lose control over much of the messaging and design. After carefully crafting his own brand image, he wasn't ready to hand it off.

So Joe and his team took the books into their own hands, writing the manuscripts quickly and partnering with Greenleaf Book Group to bring them to market on a much tighter timeline while holding on to their creative oversight. Hustling the publication of the books helped Joe stay in front of his audience and create a deeper connection with them versus disappearing after the documentary had run its course. More importantly, the books became a tool to provide his audience with extremely useful content—recipes, how-tos, and inspiration—that drove home the heart of Joe's big idea more fully.

When I encounter authors who don't understand the value of maintaining the rights to their content, I often share Joe's story with them. Because Joe chose a publishing model without restrictions on how he could use his content, he was able to take control of his larger intellectual property strategy and use it to better serve his idea. Joe owns and controls the documentary work he's done, the blog content, and the recipes he shares. Together, they all serve his personal brand and his greater goals; why should his book be any different?

It's my opinion that when an author's idea is on the line, the safest person to serve that idea is usually the author himself.

This book is for authors, like Joe, who intend to get the most leverage possible out of the blood, sweat, and tears that go into writing a book and launching a big idea.

WHY THOUGHT LEADERSHIP IS IMPORTANT

If Joe's story didn't quite make my point, owning a big idea in all its forms often takes the shape of thought leadership. You may be thinking, *Isn't the world of experts, influencers, and thought leaders a little overblown?*

Those words are definitely thrown around a lot, but their popularity doesn't make their place in today's media landscape any less important. Thought leaders continue to play a major role in helping readers and consumers find a voice they can trust.

Before you tackle the road map that we'll cover in this book for developing your position as a thought leader, it's important to have the *why* behind the work you will need to put in to reach that status.

Thought leaders help others make decisions

In our convenience economy, we are inundated with choices. With the whole world on the other side of our keyboard, we no longer have to settle for the fabric softener our local grocery store stocks. We can order an organic, unscented, paraben-free fabric softener online and have it delivered to our front door within the hour. We can also work with a business coach halfway across the world or watch personal training videos online. Our options are endless.

It's this paradox of choice that drives people toward thought leaders. Finding a voice in the crowd that they can trust helps people connect with the goods and services that are right for them. People who want to benefit from the juicing revolution don't have to do hours and hours of research on which juicer to buy. Joe Cross has a link to his favorite on his website.

What we often overlook about personal branding and thought leadership is that it's not about building the number of followers you have. It's about building connection. In today's crowded information landscape, that connection is priceless.

The strongest thought leaders wield tremendous influence because they build connections with their audience, not because they magically racked up (bought) two million social media followers. They regularly show their passion for a topic and freely share their knowledge. Moreover, they listen to and engage with their audience in return.

J. K. Rowling, for instance, famously responds to tweets from fans and answers their questions about *Harry Potter* plots.

Paulo Coelho is the author of *The Alchemist*, a *New York Times* bestseller for over 300 weeks.[1] Coelho has been blogging for years, posting at least twice a week with a range of content from stories to commentary, all helping to continue to build his audience and keep them close.

I often tell authors who balk at the idea of building a brand as a thought leader that it fundamentally just means finding your readers and customers and talking *with* them. Not so intimidating, is it?

Building that trust in a noisy, overcrowded space isn't easy, but once they have earned it, thought leaders carry tremendous influence.

Thought leaders drive change

Occasionally, thought leaders get a bad rap for being too focused on making money, and some thought leaders successfully earn their audience's trust but quickly squander it by not bringing them anything of value.

In my experience, however, these types of would-be thought leaders are uncommon. Far more often, I meet people who truly want to make

---

1   Lisa Capretto, "Paulo Coelho Explains How *The Alchemist* Went from Flop to Record-Breaking Bestseller," Video, *Huffington Post*, September 4, 2014, http://www.huffingtonpost. com/2014/09/04/the-alchemist-paulo-coelho-oprah_n_5762092.html.

an impact on the world and other people. They have vast knowledge and experience on a given topic and see how that knowledge can benefit others.

In these cases thought leadership is the vehicle through which they share their message. The more people they reach through articles, keynote speeches, social media, or media interviews, the more people they are potentially helping.

Going back to Joe Cross as an example, his big-picture goal was to help people adopt a plant-based diet and lead healthier lives. In one of his books, he shares transformation pictures from some of his readers, demonstrating how they have changed physically as a result of Joe's ideas.

This also extends to the leadership coach who is helping organizations function more efficiently or the philanthropist trying to raise awareness for a cause. Thought leaders have a powerful opportunity to impact the lives and careers of their audiences, and while many of the steps we discuss in the book are indeed focused on earning income, it's important to remember the *why* behind the effort.

It's hard to put an ROI (return on investment) figure on changing someone's life.

Thought leaders take control of their future

We've established that thought leadership can do great things for the audience it serves. But another reason thought leadership is important is that it brings opportunities to the thought leader.

Have you had days when you've thought, *Wouldn't it be nice to work on my own schedule?* Or, in my case, *Wouldn't it be nice to work from Fiji?*

In our modern "gig economy" of freelancers and four-hour-work-week enthusiasts we've seen a surge of people whose businesses are built around them, personally. They are often one-person shops, though some have figured out how to scale. Their lifestyle helps them take long sabbaticals, work remotely when they choose, or simply have more time to spend with their families.

Earning that lifestyle takes a lot of work though. You can't just hang a "thought leader" shingle on your door and head to Fiji. (Well, you can, but it won't go as planned.) It will require significant hustle to build your following, but you will certainly have more control over your schedule and your future growth than you would in a standard nine-to-five job.

ARE YOU READY TO WRITE?

Whether you're an established thought leader or you're just starting out, a published book is the cornerstone of establishing yourself as an expert. This idea is the primary focus of this book.

Writing a book is a significant investment of time, energy, and, in most cases, money. How do you know if you're ready to take the leap?

Here are six questions to ask yourself before you dive in. Later in this book, we'll revisit this conversation at a deeper, more quantitative level. For now, I encourage you to grab a notebook to jot down your answers for easy reference as we work through the process of developing your book idea.

What do you want to write about?

If the answer doesn't immediately come to you, that's okay. I'll help you work through that in this book. Most authors start with a vague idea, like "marketing tactics," and build from there. Focus on your experience and your successes to get the ball rolling.

Once you have the idea in place, create a brainstorm document where you can list some more specific topics that you feel comfortable talking about—perhaps the things that others ask you for advice or insight on. Don't worry about outlining just yet. We'll cover that later. The key here is defining a general *something* to say.

What do you want your book to accomplish?

Plenty of authors use their book as a calling card to drum up business, but you don't need to be a business owner to use writing a book to your advantage.

Are you an aspiring speaker, hoping to use your book to get your foot in the door for more corporate keynotes? Perhaps you're an executive who wants to build a personal brand outside of your company's brand? Maybe you simply want to be recognized as a writer with a book that sells well.

There is no wrong answer here, but it's important to think through your goals for the book before you get too far down the road. Publishing a book is a big investment of your time and money, and clarifying your goals will help ensure that you don't waste either one.

Who is your audience? Are you already talking to them?

Visualize and describe your target reader. Try to get in their minds before you begin writing. What are their pain points? What are they hoping to learn? Where do they get stuck? How can you help them?

This is such an important part of writing a consistent, targeted book that Greenleaf Book Group's branding team regularly creates audience profiles to help authors answer these questions. They create personas for two to three different kinds of readers that are likely to need an author's particular book. (Visit ideasinfluenceandincome.com for examples of these personas.)

While you may not need to spend hours researching these personas just yet, you can get a head start by thinking about your current platform. What kinds of followers do you have on social media? Who shares the articles you write? Chances are that you are already producing content in some way. Who is reading and engaging with it?

If you aren't actively engaging with an audience, start now. Dip your toe in the water with shorter-form works like blog posts. This will help you understand the person you are writing for, and it will also help ensure a base of demand for your book when it comes out.

Why you?

You now know what you want to say and whom you're saying it for, so it's time for an honest evaluation of why you're the best person to deliver the message.

What qualifies you to write a book on the topic you've chosen? Have you worked in the industry for years? Did you pioneer something new?

Do you have an exceptional track record of success with your methodology? Or did you do a *lot* of research on this topic?

What would be missing if someone else wrote a book on this subject?

This question will also help you identify your differentiation. What do you bring to the table that is different from the content that readers can get through existing articles, books, podcasts, white papers, and so on?

Why now?

Is there currently a demonstrated demand for your area of expertise? Are your clients increasingly asking for more information about a particular area of your business? Do you foresee a shift in the industry due to technology, politics, or economic trends?

Most nonfiction books intend to provide timely, useful content for readers, but if you are able to anticipate their *future* pain points and help them avoid certain problems in the first place, your book will gain a powerful competitive edge.

You know your industry better than most, so spend some serious time thinking about its future path to understand how you can be the go-to, long-term resource for your audience in your specific area of knowledge.

Is a book the best outlet for this idea?

Between videos, blogs, social media, white papers, articles, and so on, there are many ways to share ideas and test an audience's interest. If you have answered the first five questions in this section, challenge yourself with this one: Could I sum up everything that I want to say in a blog post? A blog series? A series of tweets?

Many readers can point to a book that contained 30 pages of valuable information and then drifted off into repetition and "fluff" for the remaining 150 pages. Before you embark on the journey of writing a book, know that you are so passionate and opinionated about your topic that you are bursting with valuable information, anecdotes, case studies, and advice.

Repurposing existing content is a helpful way to compile your book, but if you don't have enough to say to fill a book, think through your audience's needs and draft some short-form material. Get your work out there in other formats, and your voice and content will come together with time.

A book is an exceptionally valuable brand asset for a reason—it's hard work to write and successfully launch one. Working through your answers to these questions will make the process of writing easier and will be helpful at many points down the road during the publishing process.

UNDERSTAND YOUR PUBLISHING OPTIONS *EARLY*

If you've determined at this point that a book may be the logical next step for you, it's important to understand your publishing options from the outset. If you are inclined to self-publish, you'll need to approach the development of your book with the understanding that you will be handling all of the moving parts. On the other hand, if you know you want a traditional deal, your primary focus will be on the manuscript and the development of your platform. A hybrid author will, as the name implies, fall somewhere in between.

There are three basic models for publishing: self-publishing (including digital publishing), traditional publishing, and hybrid publishing. We'll get into the pros and cons of each model later in this book. We'll also provide some guidance on deciding which option is right for you, but for now, we'll give an overview of these three basic models.

Traditional publishing

With this option, the author sells publication rights to a publishing house and receives an advance, and possibly royalty payments, in return. This negotiation is usually done by means of a literary agent, who has relationships with editors and takes a portion of the advance and royalty in exchange for their help.

Since the publisher is fronting the costs and is carrying most of the risk, the typical author has less control over the process.

Self-publishing

Self-publishing has enjoyed tremendous growth in the past decade, lauded by many as the democratization of publishing. Under this model, the bulk (if not all) of the work—writing, producing, marketing, and launching the book—falls to the author.

Most self-published authors use online platforms to publish and distribute their work. The author's ownership and sweat equity bring the benefit of full creative control and the highest possible cut of book sales profit, but distribution reach is limited (bookstores are reluctant to deal with one-off authors due to administrative issues), and the publishing process can be overwhelming.

Self-published books have less stigma than they've ever had in the past, but they still carry a reputation for amateur quality because, unfortunately, that's exactly what many of them are: amateur quality. Most self-published authors work in a vacuum and handle all aspects of the publishing process, from writing to editing, design, marketing, branding, and sales. It's a rare person who can handle all of these areas with the professional quality expected by booksellers and readers.

Hybrid publishing

Hybrid publishing models are relatively new (Greenleaf Book Group, the first hybrid publisher, was founded in 1997), at least when compared to the age of the publishing industry.

While no two hybrids function exactly the same, they all blend elements of traditional publishing and self-publishing. For example, Greenleaf provides editorial and design work and actively pitches titles to national retailers (similar to traditional publishers) while allowing authors to keep their rights and collaborate in the creative process (similar to self-publishing).

Each option has benefits and drawbacks, meaning all authors should take some time to explore this choice from the perspective of their individual goals and priorities.

WHY DOES HYBRID PUBLISHING FIT FOR SO MANY THOUGHT LEADERS?

I'm writing this book because I have over a decade's worth of experience helping thought leaders develop and publish their work in a hybrid model. It is a popular choice for authors whose intellectual property is also their livelihood, due to the benefits of ownership, creative control, speed to market, and higher royalties.

It's not the right choice for everyone, especially those averse to taking risks. But if you're reading this book because you are committed to developing a thought leader brand, it's a model that your peers have adopted en masse for good reason.

To illustrate the importance of a model that allows authors to control their work, consider that in Greenleaf's hybrid structure, authors maintain full rights to their content. This means there are no hoops to jump through if they want to monetize their content in a new way, whether that's in a keynote speech, an online learning course, a workshop training program, a documentary, or a stuffed animal collection.

You get the idea. People learn and consume content in different ways. If your ideas are your livelihood, you will be best positioned to monetize them when you have full ownership and control of their use.

DO I NEED A LITERARY AGENT?

A frequent and early question in publishing is "Do I need a literary agent?" The answer depends on your goals, genre, resources, and which of the aforementioned publishing options you choose.

If you are pursuing a traditional publishing deal, an agent is essential. Most traditional publishers don't accept unsolicited manuscripts, meaning that they only accept manuscripts they've commissioned or that are represented by a reputable agent. Not only does the agent act as the middleman—and the first line of defense for the hundreds of slush submissions that publishers would otherwise have to sift through—the agent also acts on your behalf in the negotiation process when a publisher is ready to purchase the rights to your book.

If you are either self-publishing or directly pursuing an independent publisher, an agent is probably not necessary. If you are self-publishing, there is no advance to negotiate and no submissions process to get through, eliminating the need for a middleman. Independent publishers often accept submissions from authors and contract directly with them. They typically don't require a third party to represent you in any part of the process—though you should always have a lawyer take a look at all contracts before you sign.

If you've decided a literary agent is the way to go, do your homework to learn the best way to approach the agent and how to identify which ones represent your genre. Start by checking out Querytracker.net and Jeff Herman's eponymous *Jeff Herman's Guide to Book Publishers, Editors, & Literary Agents*.

If working with an agent makes sense for you, know that finding the agent who is right for you will take time. Publishing is as much about personal preference as it is about quality writing—which makes it essential that you take the time to find an agent who truly gets you and who will be an enthusiastic advocate and advisor for you and your work.

THE POWER OF AN IDEA

Striving to establish yourself as a thought leader shows that you are fully committed to your area of expertise—so much so that you are driven to share your enthusiasm with others. At times, it may feel as if you're indulging your own ego. That's okay. In fact, it's appropriate. The dictionary defines ego as "the 'I' or self of any person; a person as thinking, feeling, and willing, and distinguishing itself from the selves of others and from objects of its thought." That's exactly what we're chasing here. Give your ego a hug (it will need it once the marketing grind begins), and carry on. You're embarking on important work that will cement your brand and impact the lives of others.

As you work through the six questions designed to determine if you're ready to write, bear in mind that those questions are oriented around writing a book. You may decide that you're not ready to write a book (or maybe you're ready to write but not ready to deal with the marketing hustle that comes after that) but that you are ready to tackle shorter form essays, blogs, or even videos to fire up your content machine. In that case, I commend you for recognizing that early on and committing to use content in a way that works for you. This book will still be an excellent resource as you work through the processes of creating and executing your work.

Finally, while it is helpful to know which publishing option you are leaning toward and whether you'll need an agent on the front end, if the answer doesn't jump out at you right away, don't obsess over figuring this out while your creative juices are flowing. Writing a book can be a slog, so if the writing muse visits, honor her and write without concern for how your words will eventually reach readers. It can all be sorted out later.

We've touched on the lasting impact that a thought leader can have on an audience, but it's worth taking a moment to reflect on the power of ideas in general.

Ideas are the seeds that grow into innovations and movements that change the world. Where would we be without computers? Or the batteries and electricity they require? How about the concept of human rights? Ideas don't have to manifest as physical things to have a massive impact on our world.

These big ideas were groundbreaking. But as every businessperson can attest, timing is everything. There's a special magic when an idea sparks at a time when you are ready to embrace it and all of the outside factors that impact it align in your favor.

When these elements line up, the potential of your work increases exponentially. So when an idea hits under these conditions, seize it and do everything in your power to grind away at it and bring it to life.

Chapter 2

LETTING GO OF FEAR

You must do the things you think you cannot do.
—Eleanor Roosevelt

IN THE TWELVE-PLUS YEARS that I've been working with authors and would-be authors, the second-biggest roadblock I've seen standing between them and a final manuscript is a fear of sharing their ideas (more on the single biggest roadblock in a moment). Whether it's rooted in a fear of rejection, a fear of someone stealing the idea outright, or some combination of the two, many people use sheltering an idea as an excuse to keep the hard work associated with launching it relegated to the back burner.

Here's the deal. You can sit on your ideas and dream about their potential, crossing your fingers and hoping that, in the meantime, someone else won't skip into the picture to steal the exact title and tagline you dreamed up, or you can make a plan to cope with and move past the fears that are holding you back.

Fear of failure is a real and multidimensional force. Sometimes, we fear failure because having a dream gives us hope, and if we make our dream a reality but it fails, it feels as if hope will be gone from our lives. Other times, failure takes the form of criticism, whether from the reading public or an editor.

If your fear of failure is really a fear of losing hope, stop for a moment and take stock of all of the reasons why you are writing a book. Your effort to share your expertise with others is rooted in a desire to help them achieve their goals, to help them learn from what you've experienced, and to earn the respectable income that comes along with that deep knowledge and impact. If you empower one person, your hope may be fulfilled.

Of course, impacting one person is not the point of all of this work. We're trying to impact many. So let's think of fear of failure from a business angle, as a start-up founder would. Anyone who studies this space knows that a typical start-up pattern includes a pivot or two around value proposition and sometimes around entire product launches. A founder may intend to bring the "Uber for pet grooming" to the market, only to conduct market research and then find out that the market really wants an "Uber for pet walking." The founder does not throw in the towel. Instead, this is when their team returns to the drawing board to process and act on this fresh audience feedback.

That's exactly what you should do if you launch your idea to a lukewarm response. You can test your content on a blog to find the material that resonates, or you can try your hand at a few keynote addresses with your local chamber of commerce or the like before you commit your ideas to a manuscript. Even post-launch, you can massage the messaging around your book through fresh public relations pitching angles and marketing language.

Just like the start-up founder, you can pivot on your content and continue iterating toward its success.

Fear of failure is often really a fear of not knowing what you'll do if things don't work out as planned. Work through the answers to that. This book will help you create a well-developed manuscript. However, if your audience doesn't respond to your work as planned, you'll pivot and find a new path—and you will use the work you did to write your book (and the feedback that came from it) as a foundation to iterate on that next step. We'll talk more about repurposing your content in the *Influence* section.

With fear of failure behind us, we are left to contend with criticism and editors. Criticism is an editor's handmaiden, so the two overlap a bit—but dealing with each experience is quite different.

THE FEAR OF CRITICISM

Sharing your idea early on is important to its success for a number of reasons. First, you need feedback to refine both your idea and how you talk about or pitch it. Entrepreneurs understandably hold a personal bias of favor toward their own ideas. You have to, or you wouldn't have the confidence to launch it! But sometimes we make the mistake of projecting our own preferences onto a wider audience that actually does not share the interest we hold. The best way to catch that early enough to shift gears is to begin bouncing your idea off of trusted parties well before launch, using their feedback to retool where necessary if you encounter confusion about the pitch or a general lack of enthusiasm.

You also need support and a strong network, so holding back on sharing your idea can mean missing out on opportunities for partnerships, collaborations, recruiting, and even investor interest.

Last but not least, speaking your ideas aloud to others creates a certain level of accountability. Many of us are more apt to follow through on something once we've made our intentions known to others. If you're tipping toward the nonstarter side of things, start by telling a few trusted family members about what you're working on.

A good way to strike a balance between the fear of sharing ideas and the need for feedback is to focus on sharing the *why*, not the *how*. What problem are you solving for your audience? What need does your audience have that you fill? Remember, execution is the magic behind a successful launch . . . and outside of investors, most people don't care to hear about how you're doing what you're doing. They really want to know what you're doing that will make their life easier or better.

This is also a good reason to use the pitch technique of comparing your idea to a known entity—"It's like Yelp for creative services." You save having to explain how the functional part of the business works and are just focusing on the new angle and market served.

In the words of Anatole France, "It is by acts and not by ideas that people live." Your ideas are seeds; feedback and execution are the light and water that make them thrive.

Fear of criticism (how to handle, when to listen, when to dismiss, reality of bad reviews) is often overwhelming. Writing can be a downright scary process. Whether you're writing a book or an article, you are opening your ideas to an audience and allowing them to engage—and maybe criticize—your work.

For this reason, writers often hold their content close and only allow others to read it when it feels polished and complete.

The downside to keeping your ideas and writing private lies in losing out on valuable feedback if you don't share early and with the right people. Without early feedback, you might find that entire chapters of your book need to be reworked because you hadn't thought through a concept completely. Now you'll need to spend as much time correcting your mistake as you did writing the initial draft.

Once you've started opening up, beware the temptation to listen to everyone's feedback equally. Recognize that feedback can come in many forms, and if you take all suggestions to heart, your own voice and message may get lost.

When you're ready to dive into your next writing project, keep these ideas in mind to ensure that you're getting the *right* kind of feedback before it's too late.

THE FEAR OF EDITORS

Fearing negative feedback from readers is logical, because you're writing your book for them. After all the work that goes into writing and promoting a book, it's understandable that one negative bit of reader feedback might sit with you far longer than ten positive instances of feedback—a phenomenon I've witnessed with my authors often.

Fearing the feedback of an editor is not so logical, and yet, it's a reality that many writers face. While it's true that you're putting yourself in a position of vulnerability by opening up your work for this early feedback, it's important to remember that your editor is a partner. Here are a few points about working with an editor to make the idea a bit easier to swallow.

Your editor wants to make you look good

Editors are unsung heroes in the publishing world. Their work requires extensive knowledge of language, the ability to put themselves in both the writers' and readers' shoes, a remarkable level of patience, and an undying passion for supporting the art of the written word.

These champions of writing want to serve as your support team, not as nitpicking overlords. Editing is typically a collaborative process. In self-publishing and hybrid models, it is especially collaborative since the author bears most of the risk and creative control. But even in traditional models, the experienced editor understands that this is *your* book and will offer both positive and critical feedback.

Your editor is a proxy for the reader

Your editor will review your work with one person in mind, and it's not you. It's your reader.

Have you ever had an investment professional review your portfolio to make suggestions on how you're using your resources? Your investment advisor is thinking about how to make your money perform well in the market, which benefits you.

To use that analogy, your editor is reviewing the investment you've made in words to make sure it will perform well in the market (readers), which also benefits you.

An editor makes suggestions to make a better book, not to criticize your chops as a writer. Don't take their feedback personally! It's the editor's challenge to serve as the objective outside eyes of your reader, who may be considering your idea or concept for the first time. The reader's worldview, experience, and sophistication around the content area you've mastered are probably levels below yours. Otherwise, they'd be writing the book, not reading it.

That makes the editor's work incredibly important. As an expert, it's hard for you to remember what it's like to experience your area of knowledge as a layman. You may take for granted that your audience understands certain concepts, acronyms, and industry norms or trends. But to reach and impact the right audience(s), you'll often need to take a step back and retool your writing so it's effective for an audience with a different perspective than yours. This is a process that definitely requires solid editorial help.

Fit matters

Given the vulnerability involved in putting your writing in front of an editor and the importance of their work, it's critical that you feel this person is a trusted partner who understands your voice and purpose.

Authors sometimes wince at editorial expenses, but this is an area where you get what you pay for. If I had a nickel for every author who told me their book was already edited and then realized they needed more editorial work after receiving a proper review from an experienced editorial team . . . Well, I won't say I'd be rich, but I'd definitely buy you all drinks.

Respect the work you've done and give it a fighting chance by bringing a seasoned editor on board to refine it.

Be prepared for the redline

Close your eyes for a second and think back to your high school or college years. Do you remember a particular paper you had to write, whether it was a creative or critical piece, and how worried you were about your professor's feedback?

That feedback probably came back in the form of red ink all over your precious work, or perhaps a digital version of the same.

The thing about redlines and edits or comments made in tracked changes is that the initial optics can be overwhelming. Your eyes take in the *quantity* of edits, not the nature of the edits. So if you were taught to double space after a period and your editor corrects that to a single space throughout, your manuscript might look like an absolute mess at first glance. But upon a more careful review, you'll realize that you're dealing with a mechanical concern and not a content issue—much easier to resolve!

Don't be overwhelmed by the optics of your redline review. Your editor should offer some summary feedback on the nature of the major changes and should also advise if there's a mechanical error pattern in the manuscript (akin to a double space after a period) that has created edits throughout. A quick phone call to discuss the editorial feedback can be very helpful in terms of reviewing it with context and a vision for how the change will improve the final product.

FEAR OF IDEA THIEVES

Like authors, entrepreneurs exist in a community powered by creativity and ideas. Also like authors, entrepreneurs can be hamstrung by fear and distrust. This fear often extends past the fear of criticism; they often fear that someone will steal their intellectual property (IP).

The first thing I tell an author in this fear mindset is to bear in mind that the power of an idea lies in its execution. This is also true in business. The single biggest roadblock between an idea and its launch is the failure to execute at all, as in not even start. And the people who *are* good at starting are, you guessed it, knee-deep in launching something of their own, leaving little time to spend on stealing others' ideas.

Moving past the nonstarters, the power of execution also refers to the unique approach that you and your experience bring to the table. There are countless combinations of approaches to constructing business models, product launches, marketing strategies, branding, company culture, and so on—but only one combination that you would choose based on your experience and philosophies. You and your background are part of your competitive advantage.

Another point to consider is that if your idea is that easy for someone to steal, you may have a different issue on your hands. Something that is easy to rip off and implement without your guidance, knowledge, connections, and so forth may have difficulty holding on to market share. In most cases, you'll be better served in the long run by taking the time to understand your market and create a better product. You don't necessarily need to be first to market to be successful. Often, as the saying goes, the pioneers get the arrows and the settlers get the land.

Naturally, you don't want to share your content with just anyone. Being strategic about who you bring into your feedback circle will also help to allay the fear of being ripped off.

Who you want to share your content with

It's a common inclination to want to share any new project with the people who we're closest to in life, whether that's a spouse, a proud parent, or a friend.

These are also the people most likely to shower us with praise, whether or not it's warranted.

As often as people advise avoiding this route at all costs, it can have its benefits in certain situations. Dad may not know the ins and outs of your topic, but he may be one of your biggest supporters and can give the encouragement you need to push past writer's block or fear.

Just remember that if you're sharing your writing with someone because you're looking for support, it's okay to tune out their ancillary feedback.

Who you need to share your content with

When you start a writing project, develop a list of people whose opinions you trust and who know your content well. This could include colleagues, peers, mentors, or experienced editors.

You need some people who will tell it to you straight, unlike your supportive dad. Those who understand your goals and topic are better equipped to evaluate your ideas, challenge them, ask thought-provoking questions, and ultimately save you time and effort during the revision process.

Authors who work with an editor who is familiar with their field throughout the outlining and brainstorming process have a clearer understanding of their path forward and can finish writing more quickly. They are also less likely to be derailed later when they start promoting the book and inevitably receive critical feedback.

What to do with the feedback

When you get early feedback, be grateful and take the time to listen to it, no matter where it comes from. Someone who shares their ideas with you is engaged, and often, it also means that they're invested in your success.

That said, remember the kinds of feedback you're seeking. Does the feedback help propel you forward? Did it unlock a different angle you hadn't considered yet?

Mentally classify that feedback to help avoid spending too much time on unnecessary overthinking and self-criticism

Work through any feedback that challenged you. If possible, schedule time with the person who brought that feedback to you so that you can turn their ideas over at a deeper level and weigh the possibility of integrating their points into your work.

Consider feedback as an ongoing, natural part of being a creator. Once your ideas go public, you'll receive it whether or not you ask for it.

Fear is a legitimate factor that can come between you and a completed book. It manifests in many forms, all of which you can overcome with the right mindset and tools to mitigate its stalling effects. With these tips, you'll learn to embrace rather than fear early feedback in all its forms and, more importantly, to manage it in a way that is beneficial to you.

Fear often surfaces from a lack of preparation or certainty around the mission at hand. In the next chapter, we'll tackle some big questions that hold the golden answers to help us preempt fear and replace it with confidence and vision.

Chapter 3

IDENTIFYING YOUR BRAND

Price is what you pay. Value is what you get.
—Warren Buffet

THROUGHOUT THIS BOOK, YOU'LL BE REMINDED of the importance of creating a differentiated message in an authentic voice and of the ongoing work required to build an audience for that message. Don't make the mistake of thinking that you can write a book, sit back, and let the readers make it into a hit from there. Particularly with nonfiction, this rarely happens. Breakout nonfiction titles are the product of strong content, strong brands, strong distribution, and strong marketing strategies.

Before you begin work on your manuscript, you'll need to work through the answers to questions around differentiation, potential markets, and competitive products, and, of course, you'll need a watertight pitch about the value of your content. This is a worthwhile exercise even if you choose to self-publish and never intend to engage an agent or publisher. The stronger your pitch, the more in tune you'll be with your message and the value your book provides.

When thinking about your brand, I encourage you to ask yourself what problem you are solving, why, and for whom.

The answers to these questions will lay the foundation for your writing and marketing strategies. The more heavy lifting you do on the front end to get clear on your messaging, the easier it will be to maintain and sustain that work on an ongoing basis. Hammering out a brand blueprint and committing the energy to fully understand it will give you the context you need to not only focus your writing work but also eventually manage interviews, social media posts, and even partnerships with a consistent audience and goal in mind.

WHO IS YOUR AUDIENCE?

Job number one as an author is to know your audience and write to their needs. If you do this well, your writing and branding will be more intentional, useful, and relevant—which will underpin more successful content overall.

Of course, a critical part of defining a brand is to understand who the readers of your book are, both in qualitative and quantitative terms.

What kind of people are your potential readers

To start, try to build a clear profile of your targeted reader. The more conclusions you can draw around their demographics, their lifestyle, their goals, their passions, and so on, the easier it will be for you to churn out content that strongly resonates with them. It's important to tackle this question from both quantitative and qualitative viewpoints, as each perspective will provide information that will help to guide both your creative and business decisions.

To determine who your audience is in qualitative terms, ask yourself these questions:

- Who would be interested in this topic?
- Where do they live?
- What kind of work do they do?
- What are their hobbies?
- How do they currently get this information?

And so on.

The key is to be as specific as possible. It's not enough to say your book is geared toward "businesspeople." Instead of "businesspeople," you could say "middle managers of Fortune 500 companies" or "solopreneurs in the retail sector." This may help you identify marketing opportunities for your book, and it will also help the publishing team cultivate your content so that it speaks to and meets the needs of your audience.

As you work through this process, you will probably define your primary audience fairly quickly. As an expert in your field, you're well acquainted with the type of person you've learned to orient your work around. Below your primary audience, however, you will have secondary and even tertiary audiences whose separate demographic profiles will require different marketing strategies down the road (and who open up additional opportunities and pipelines for you!).

For example, this book is primarily written for nonfiction authors. Beyond that, it would be useful for professional content marketers working in a corporate environment. Another audience for this book might be found in communications students who hope to use this information to further their own work one day. Each of these audiences will require different messaging, marketing, and even distribution strategies, so the earlier they are defined, the better we can plan to incorporate them into our launch plan.

How many potential readers

Quantitative information is a bit more time-consuming to locate but can be valuable in determining the strength and validity of your topic or idea. If you have a large number of potential readers, publishers will consider a project more favorably. Specialty or niche topics that appeal to a smaller group are more difficult to place with a publishing house and are even more difficult to distribute nationally. To help you, here are some resources for locating numbers on specific groups:

- Visit the US Department of Labor's Bureau of Labor Statistics at bls.gov. There you can locate all kinds of statistics related to the economy and workforce at regional, national, and international levels.
- Contact organizations that serve your market, and ask for data on the size and demographic nature of their membership.
- Identify the top magazines that your audience reads. Go to their advertisers page. They typically offer an advertiser's kit that includes audience size and demographics.

Of course, confirming that a potential readership exists en masse is no guarantee of book sales if you don't have a plan to reach them. But selling books is a numbers game to some degree, so use the quantitative information to inform and prioritize your marketing plan when that time comes.

Digging into this qualitative and quantitative information will help you make smarter decisions around your messaging, marketing, and launch strategy. You also may stumble upon some data that opens your eyes to underserved markets that can benefit from your work. Organize the key findings from your research in a simple summary format for easy reference down the road, whether for your own purposes or to bring those on your team up to speed.

WHAT DOES YOUR AUDIENCE NEED FROM YOU?

The reason most nonfiction readers seek out a book on a particular topic in the first place is to build background or working knowledge in a specific subject area. Consider your own mindset the last time you purchased a book. Were you curious about the history of a global issue? Were you stuck on a business quandary without an obvious answer? Were you trying to deepen your understanding of an area where you have familiarity but not deep knowledge (for example, marketing, nutrition, or sustainability)?

The challenge or problem that drives a reader to seek your solution is their *pain point*. Just as it sounds, a pain point refers to an issue or question that keeps your reader up at night, impedes their business or personal growth, or reduces their quality of life in some way.

Be careful in assuming that you know your audience's pain points. We are sometimes too close to our own deep knowledge to understand what the layman is seeking. You may instinctively have some of these answers from your years in the field, or you may have to do some keyword research and social media polling to find the strongest need. (A little experimentation with various keywords via Google AdWords will provide a wealth of intelligence around your audience's pain points.) If you're in a position to do so, consider polling your current customers or audience to uncover the deepest possible feedback around this question. Their answers can provide a goldmine of unexpected information around effective messaging and marketing to best address their areas of need.

Why should your audience listen to you?

What do you want to communicate to your audience, and how is that message going to make their lives easier, better, more fulfilling? Warning: Getting this right requires more than thinking about what you want to say. Consider your audience and focus on what they want to hear, as aligned with your desired outcomes. It could be that you deliver results, not fluff; that you are funny; that you are experienced; or that your material or system is better than the competition's. Be disciplined and prioritize a clear communication goal. Try to capture this in one sentence (e.g., "I help working women to reconcile work-life balance issues and feel content inside and outside the home").

With outcomes and a communications goal under your belt, the next step is to inventory any existing content you've created. Turn over every rock and make a list of your content assets, including blog posts, stories or anecdotes, newsletters, white papers, presentations, books, workbooks, audio recordings, video, tests and quizzes, handouts, articles, and so on. This may take some time, but stay the course. Some people find a simple Excel matrix beneficial for categorizing numerous content assets by title, type, and length—but do whatever works for you.

Once your content is inventoried, turn back to your desired outcome and communication goals. Look at each piece of content and make a ruling on whether it supports both of those goals. That should narrow the field a bit. From there, objectively examine the content assets that made the cut to make sure they are still current and, of course, good. Don't immediately write them off if that's not the case; a little reworking can usually make a so-so piece better or bring an outdated piece up-to-date.

Quite often, a creator is too close to his or her own ideas to do this sort of objective evaluation. If you find yourself giving every piece of content the green light, consider bringing in an outside eye to bring more unbiased feedback to this process.

You've identified what you have to offer your readers, and now it's time to structure the content to carry your message forward. Quite often, this process helps experts to move beyond the surface elevator pitch of their positioning and to identify and refine the specific, actionable ways that they impact others. What tips, strategies, frameworks, and examples do you have that help communicate your message and provide value to your audience? Do you have access to important statistics, research, or fellow experts? Compile all of this information into talking points and organize them by subtopic, and then pull together supporting facts and actionable tools to help the reader apply your knowledge. Identifying these resources now will make for a smoother writing process down the road, especially as you begin your outline.

What will readers be missing out on if someone else writes this book? That may be experience you can share, your humor, or your ability to break down a complex topic to be easily understandable.

Again, don't rush this process. It may take some time to find the words that you feel you can build a brand around and live with for years to come. True thought leaders are authorities on a specific topic—and the more specific and differentiated their area of expertise, the better. Those who claim to be experts on multiple topics aren't experts at all; they're dabblers. Establishing yourself as an expert takes experience, knowledge, and a track record of results. Writing a book on that expertise cements your reputation as a thought leader in your specific area.

UNDERSTAND YOUR MARKET

Whether you're writing for brand-building purposes, for legacy reasons, or just to get it off the proverbial bucket list, you are probably also thinking about how you can assess the marketability of your book idea on the front end before investing time and effort in writing and publishing it. You are smart to do so, as the answer to the marketability question will ultimately impact your publishing option decision.

As an example, a book with a smaller niche audience may be best suited for online distribution. I often use the example of a book about how to become a pharmaceutical sales rep. It's not a book you will find stocked in a bookstore—and for good reason; its audience is small and clearly defined and will be looking for this very specific content primarily online.

In contrast, books that have a broader (or simply more popular) subject area can benefit from a traditional release that targets both online and physical retail channels. There's an interesting fine line to tread in this regard between general and niche content. Books that are too general can suffer from a lack of distinction, while books that are overly specific find a limited audience best suited for online distribution. But it's absolutely magical when a book that addresses a niche content area (paleo cooking, for example) intersects with a swell in consumer interest that creates rising general demand. Catching these trends and publishing at the proper inflection point will firmly establish these astute authors as pioneers in their fields.

This is where a publisher or distributor with direct access to buyer feedback around current retail trends can provide invaluable feedback to help guide your manuscript development or publishing route of choice. As in any industry, new publishing standouts are built on a combination of excellent product, strategic marketing, and impeccable timing.

Defining and measuring an audience and their willingness to buy may not always be so straightforward. Bloggers have an advantage here, because their blog posts serve as standalone research and development experiments. They can measure the interest in, shareability of, and engagement with each of their posts to zero in on the content with the highest impact. Similarly, I've seen authors publish magazine articles on a topic of their expertise to strong positive feedback and take a cue from that reaction to develop it into a full book.

If you already have that kind of market feedback at your fingertips, great! You've got a head start. If not, you'll need to spend some time thinking through the critical brand-oriented questions in this chapter to help determine who your audience is. Grab a notebook, and start this work now, before you polish off your manuscript, so that you don't end up rewriting it when you realize your tone is off for your intended market.

HOW DO YOU STAND OUT?

Clutter—it overwhelms us at every level. Twitter, radio, television, blogs . . . It's easy to get lost in the compost pile of media. So as the CEO of a publishing company, the $64,000 question I often hear experts and authors ask is, "How do we cut through this clutter to be seen and heard?"

The answer boils down to differentiating two things in the marketplace: you and your content.

Start by ensuring that your message is relevant and differentiated. What specific areas of your expertise do people consistently draw on? How is your approach or philosophy different from that of your closest competitors? Once you've refined your unique positioning, boil the value proposition down into a succinct elevator pitch.

Very often, this is where an author gets stuck, because it's hard for them to keep it short and stop talking about the subject they know so well. The goal is for your pitch to pique the listener's interest to the point that they become curious and ask for follow-up information. For example, Jane Doe might ramblingly describe herself as a fun-loving foodie with a thyroid issue who loves to cook for others in a way that helps them to manage their hormonal issues while still serving up delicious meals so that people with thyroid problems don't have to sacrifice their enjoyment of food due to a restrictive diet. Yeesh, that's a mouthful!

After tightening up the message to answer what she does, who she serves and why, and how she's different, it might read more like this: Jane is dedicated to helping fellow thyroid disease sufferers to understand and develop a therapeutic approach to nutrition. Through her lighthearted videos, cookbooks, and social media content, Jane demonstrates both the science and sizzle of cooking for hormonal balance.

I've seen retail buyers, literary agents, publicists, and the media make decisions on a pitch after about two sentences. If you can't explain the "brand of you" in ten seconds, your message isn't strong enough.

After you've narrowed down your specialty and differentiated yourself from your competition, you'll next identify the value that you will bring to others. Using a nonprofit leadership example, a book could establish a value proposition of "developing socially oriented leaders" or "teaching organizers how to motivate volunteers." Make a list of key messages, bring in a few trusted advisors, and begin brainstorming, creating, and refining until your stated value proposition is accurate and succinct. Being specific and brief will help you quickly hone in on your target audience, and it will help them identify you as an authority on their topic of concern. This will ultimately help you attract the right potential readers and prospective clients.

Who's your competition?

If you decide to pursue a traditional publishing deal, you'll first need to write a query letter to find an agent interested in handling your work. Next, you'll develop and pitch your book proposal. Even if you don't elect to work with an agent or a traditional publisher, developing a book proposal can serve as an excellent exercise to establish clarity around your target audience, content differentiation, marketing strategy, and other key elements behind a successful book launch. Visit ideasinfluenceandincome.com for best practices around developing a book proposal.

In a typical book proposal, you'll be expected to note the top two to three titles comparable to your work and how your book differs from them. This helps the agent or editor considering your proposal to identify the sales potential for your book and also helps the publisher identify exactly where you fit in the retail market. There are several ways you can research this information:

- Go to an independent bookstore and try to connect with the buyer responsible for the section your competitors are shelved in. (At major chains, buying is done at the corporate level, so it can be harder to find this expertise in your local store.) This person may be able to point you to the strong, consistent sellers in your category. Take notes on your competitors, their writing, and how you differ.

- Search online book retail sites to find the books closest to yours, written by authors like you. Try to identify authors who not only write on similar topics but who also have similar experience and backgrounds. A new book by an author with ten previous bestsellers is going to have a much stronger initial sales pattern than yours, so don't use it as a comparative title. These sites typically list titles by ranking and do not provide actual sales numbers, but the ranking can be telling in and of itself as long as there is some longevity to the book's success. Sales rankings are fairly easy to manipulate on a short-term basis, so in addition to ranking, it's helpful to look for books with over fifty reviews (as long as all of the reviews didn't come in on the same day, which can indicate unethical paid reviews).

- Nielsen provides a book sales reporting service called BookScan. It captures about 75–80 percent of retail book sales and is the only tool available to the publishing industry to provide sell-through figures for the bookselling retail market. Unfortunately, a subscription to BookScan is very expensive. For this reason, expect to lean on your literary agent or even your publisher (both of whom likely have BookScan access) to better understand your competition's performance in the retail market.

After you have identified the top two to three titles from each of these areas, compare them with your book. How are you different? It's critical to define this differentiation with as fine a point as you can make. Readers do not want a rehashing of existing information; they want something new and fresh. You can set yourself apart in a number of ways:

- Do you challenge any of the assumptions or strategies those authors make?

- Do you have a fresh approach or new information to add to the discussion?

- Do you have a more engaging or unique voice?

- Do you have more credibility or experience?

- Are you more specialized or more comprehensive?

Knowing the answers to these questions will also help you to further hone your overall message and brand strategy.

Would-be writers are often derailed by the struggle to understand whether there might be a market for their work. Given the level of effort required to write a book, it's important to spend this time evaluating the viability of your concept on the front end. In doing so, you will have a game plan for developing your content and the confidence that your time writing is well spent.

Some authors see this work as "nice to have" time for, but you really do "need to have" (or make) time to work through these questions on the front end of the publishing process. Rest assured that it will pay off in the form of consistency and efficiency gained from having the many players involved in launching a book all rowing in the same direction.

Identify category or genre

Understanding the category, or genre, that will be listed on your book can help you to stay focused on your target audience throughout the creative process. Unfortunately, most authors don't think about this until a publisher or distributor asks for this information. Most new authors (especially those who self-publish without the guidance of industry experts) commit one or all of the following category crimes in their proposals or even their finished book:

- Listing the wrong category on the cover or in the proposal
- Using descriptive terms instead of industry standard category names (like making up *teamwork* as a category instead of *business & economics/management*)

The category designation serves an essential purpose in retail distribution and should not be taken lightly. It governs your book's location, whether that ultimately means it is on a shelf or in an online database. Either way, it is essential for discoverability and will help guide your writing and marketing efforts. Here are three tips to help you choose the right categories for your book.

USE BISAC SUBJECT CODES

A BISAC (Book Industry Standards and Communications) subject code is not necessary in a book proposal, but researching yours on the front end will help you gain clarity on how your book will be positioned in retail systems from a category perspective. BISAC codes represent major categories like self-help, business & economics, parenting, and art, as a few examples. Many of the major headings also have subcategories for popular content areas, such as business & economics/budgeting. Many of the systems that wholesalers, distributors, and retailers use to set up titles require a BISAC subject code, and you can use these codes to help you determine the most appropriate category to include in your proposal or on your book cover.

When selecting your title's BISAC subject code(s), consider the audience you will be marketing to and the content of the work. Gather some objective opinions from people outside the project, and research the classification of similar titles.

If your title closely matches two different subjects, choose the one you think your target audience is most likely to use when looking for it. Keep in mind, however, that booksellers' cataloging departments may override your subject listing if it doesn't fit within their shelving systems.

The full list of BISAC codes is available at bisg.org.

DISCUSS CATEGORY CHOICES WITH YOUR AGENT, PUBLISHER, OR DISTRIBUTOR

Some books legitimately straddle genres. This happens frequently in categories like self-help and business/motivation. An agent or distributor may have reason to think that one editor or buyer will react better to your book than another and may suggest a category based on that understanding. This decision could have a huge impact on an agent's ability to negotiate a deal or a distributor's ability to negotiate for big sales and good store placement. It's better to know this before you finish writing the book versus having to retool the tone after you thought you were done with your manuscript.

CONSIDER LOCATION, LOCATION, LOCATION

Your book's category defines not only your audience but also the location of its placement in databases and bookstores. Remember that a physical book cannot live simultaneously in business, fiction, and self-help, so choose its main category in terms of the location that is the most desirable in terms of audience and most appropriate for its content.

Establishing your brand will help ensure success

Working through the answers to these questions may feel like a waste of time, especially if you're excited to just dig in on the writing itself. I assure you, it is not a waste of time. It's hard work that will give you a competitive advantage as you launch your book. As we move into the latter sections of this book, you'll begin to get a more complete picture of how challenging it can be to bring attention to your message. This foundational work gives you both a roadmap to develop a better product and a brand resource to guide the many initiatives that will follow the launch of the book itself.

Trust the process and commit to giving your book a fighting chance by tackling these branding and messaging questions. The stronger your understanding is of your audience, your competition, the market, and your own positioning, the better set up you'll be to succeed as you launch your book. Pull together a trusted team to help you stay objective and to provide the accountability to finish out this work.

Remember, a book launch is a product launch requiring all of the preparation and planning found behind any successful product launch. Creative products aren't exempt from planning and strategy needs. If anything, they require even more focus in those areas. As writers, we can become emotionally attached to our books and easily lapse into magical thinking like *I worked so hard on this book; surely it will be a success!* Your readers don't know or care how hard writing a book was for you. They care about whether or not you cure a pain point. Double down on that focus, and refuse to compromise when it comes to serving your audience and their needs.

Chapter 4

SUPPORTING THE CREATIVE PROCESS

I hate writing. I love having written.
—Dorothy Parker

BY NOW, YOU UNDERSTAND THAT, for even the most efficient authors, writing a book is hard work. Fortunately, you can make the process a bit easier on yourself with strategy, tools, and resources to help you get a jumpstart (or a push) through the most challenging areas.

Bear in mind that the creative process may not pan out as you envisioned back when your book idea was an exciting spark of an idea. No worries. Adjust, adapt, and call in help to keep the momentum moving forward. There's no prize for Most Arduous Writing Process. Take advantage of every tool and opportunity that helps you stay on track as you develop your manuscript.

REPURPOSING YOUR CONTENT

One of the most important takeaways from this book should be the power of repurposing content. Whether you started as a blogger and want to roll that content into a book, or you did the opposite and want to deconstruct your book into smaller standalone pieces, reusing your content is one of the smartest ways to leverage your ideas to create influence and, ultimately, income.

Before you start writing your book, you should scour your creative archives for content you might already have (assuming the rights to that content are free and clear or can be easily acquired). Many business authors start by writing articles and white papers for business magazines and journals. These can often be used outright, or with permission from the publication that first published the work, as meaningful parts of your book.

Authors sometimes hesitate to leverage their existing content, because they fear their reader will see the same work twice. Should you be so lucky! The truth is that, for most of us, any article we are able to place with a publication (online or print) will only reach a small fraction of our potential audience. More importantly, even if you do reach the same audience twice, readers rarely hang on to enough detail from an article to recognize it years later as a part of a larger work. Perhaps they'll remember the concept, but it's not likely to strike them as duplicative when presented within the larger context of your book.

When sifting through content you've already created to find pieces that fit into your book, look for the following qualifying elements.

Timeless content

Blog posts are often tied to current events or trends by design, but your book should contain more "evergreen" content that doesn't age or expire alongside fast-changing subjects like technology and politics. For various reasons related to updating editions, changing files, and possibly reprinting books, it's most effective to avoid timely topics in your book. That commentary can be used on your blog or social media instead.

It fits in your outline

You'll have a stronger book if you start with an outline that demonstrates a logical flow and progression for the reader to learn what you want to share. Look for places where your existing content fits and can serve that larger purpose.

Avoid dumping all of your content onto the proverbial table and trying to create a through line to connect it all in an effort to avoid writing anything new. This can be done (and has been), but it will result in a disjointed book without a strong and consistent theme. Your reader will sense the choppiness unless your content is incredibly consistent in tone and magically flows together to support one larger promise.

If you find some incredible content that just kills you to leave out because it's great but not quite a match for your outline, know that you can probably use it in your promotional efforts down the road by writing a short introduction tying it back to the larger theme of your book.

For example, with this book, I'm leaving out an article I've written about the nuts and bolts of how Nielsen's BookScan calculates retail sell-through for book products based on statistical sampling. I think it's fascinating, and it's relevant to authors, but it's a bit of a rabbit hole that doesn't directly support my goal of helping you maximize your ideas, influence, and income. Instead, I'll offer it as a guest post on another site with an intro paragraph that frames it as "the science behind one way to measure the success of a book, a topic covered at length in my new release, *Ideas, Influence, and Income.*" Tie it back to your book so your great content is still serving a purpose, even if it's in a supporting role. We'll explore outlines in more depth in the next chapter.

It's proven

If you have existing content that meets the above criteria of being timeless and on topic with your outline, ideally it's also content that has some performance metrics around clicks, engagement, views, time spent on page, and so on to help you gauge whether it's already working for your readers.

It's tempting to use any and all existing content for the sake of avoiding additional writing work, but if the content you have on a certain subject underperforms by your standards, either rework it or create something entirely new.

Be judicious about using existing content to support the message of your book. Cutting corners by reusing subpar content will certainly hurt the reader experience, and as you'll learn later in this book, every reader who picks up your book is a reader that you've worked very hard to earn and don't want to lose.

GETTING FEEDBACK

Once the outline of your book is complete, all that remains is to sit down and write. The task is straightforward enough, but for all but a rare few, the process of writing 60,000+ words is exceptionally difficult.

One of the most frequent obstacles between an author and his or her finished manuscript is feeling paralyzed by the overwhelming task. Questions about where to start, what to cover, how to structure it, and whether it's even good content can completely derail even the strongest writer.

A strong, detailed outline will be of some help in this situation because it allows you to tackle the manuscript in smaller, more manageable chunks—but sometimes the outline is not enough to keep you writing, or you may be stuck on finishing your outline. When a certain level of accountability, emotional support, or feedback might help you finish your manuscript, a writers group might be a good option—with a few caveats.

Writers groups are typically local meetings but can also occur as online groups and even at workshops and conferences on a more one-off basis. Be wary of groups that are too small or too big; fewer than five members will make it a challenge to get feedback, while a group larger than ten members will make it difficult for everyone to get a turn for feedback in one meeting.

Some writers groups are oriented more around networking and social contact, while others are structured to support manuscript development and critique. Consider your priorities, and ask the group leader or moderator about the group's purpose and approach before you make the commitment to join.

A typical in-person writers group will have more fiction than nonfiction writers, so your best bet is to find a group that will support you from an accountability standpoint. Knowing that someone is expecting you to churn out a certain number of words, or a finished outline, by the next meeting can do wonders for your productivity.

However, keep in mind that there can be a few drawbacks to using a writers group to help develop your manuscript.

Your fellow writers group members may also be working on their first manuscript. This does not make them the most qualified group to give feedback on what you're developing. The craft of creating structure, cohesion, and flow in a book is what a good editor does. A love for reading does not make someone a good editor any more than a love for music makes me a good singer (and I am not). If you choose to work within a writers group for manuscript development, be prepared to graciously accept critique but reserve final judgment for an editor's experienced eye.

Along the same lines, the content being shared for critique within a writers group is typically one portion of the manuscript, whether that's a certain number of pages or an entire chapter. For nonfiction in particular, evaluating one portion without the context of the content that precedes and follows it can lead to problems with the manuscript flow and idea development.

In light of these concerns, some authors choose to simply circulate their manuscript in progress among friends and family for critique and feedback. While feedback from those who are familiar with your subject area is always helpful, your friends and family are likely to sugarcoat their response to your work to avoid hurting your feelings or creating tension. Most people are uncomfortable giving negative feedback, and that is especially true within your closest social circles.

Speaking of negative feedback, or even constructive feedback, receive it graciously and don't argue with the person sharing their thoughts. Even if you ultimately don't act on it, all feedback is a gift and fuel for growth. You may need to ask follow-up questions to get feedback specific enough to be helpful ("Chapter three was confusing and I felt lost after that point" versus "It just didn't work for me").

And be sure to send a finished copy with a handwritten thank you note once your book is published!

ASKING FOR HELP

As you are plugging away at developing your manuscript, you'll find that some sections come easier than others. These rough spots might be due to the content itself, or they might stem from an organizational issue, or it could just be that you are too tired or preoccupied to focus.

If you're stuck because you're tired or preoccupied, jot down some concepts or keywords and try again tomorrow when you're fresh and focused.

Being stuck due to content and structure issues can become discouraging quickly. You may find yourself second-guessing everything you've written, the order in which you wrote it, and even whether the book is worth finishing.

Before you get to that level of writing fatigue, step away from the manuscript and consider bringing in an expert to help. Writing a book requires skill, and especially if this is your first time developing a manuscript, it would be unusual for you *not* to get stuck at some point. After all, you are probably not a writer by trade.

Interestingly, I work with many authors who are businesspeople "by day" and embrace the concept of hiring people to bolster areas of weakness in their companies, yet they resist bringing in editorial help to work through areas of weakness in a manuscript. They'll bring in sales and marketing staff to grow beyond what they can provide personally, but they insist on flying solo when writing.

While writing a book is a more individualistic effort, its creation deserves the same strategic resource management that running a company requires. Having a good developmental editor coaching you through the writing process is often what makes the difference between a finished manuscript and a half-written manuscript that is abandoned forever in a desk drawer out of frustration.

Having a developmental editor ride shotgun can also ensure that you don't make structural mistakes like omitting key parts of a logical content flow (especially when introducing big ideas or frameworks) or repeating content in the manuscript. Again, structuring a manuscript is a high-level editorial skill. Getting it wrong will almost certainly mean you'll have to rework and rewrite sections of your book later. If you think you have writing fatigue now, just wait until you have to rewrite what you thought was done.

Bringing in this outside help doesn't make you any less of a writer, and having that help is actually more common than not. Editors are trained to work through exactly this type of writing challenge, and you are not. You're not being a weak writer; you're being a smart writer.

I've worked with some keynote speakers who can transfix an audience from the stage but whose words fall flat on paper. They struggle to rework their writing but often fail, not immediately recognizing that the spoken word is an entirely different communication form than the written word, and mastering each requires very different skill sets. But when it comes to selecting the books we publish, I'll choose a strong speaker whose writing needs work before a strong writer who is a weak speaker. Why? I can bring in editors of all stripes to make that book shine, but I can't send anyone up on stage to save the struggling speaker. A solid team can make an average writer look amazing, but even the most stellar speaking coaches in the world can only do so much for the speaker who ultimately performs alone.

You're most likely in the strong speaker category: even if you're not speaking now, you have the passion and experience to talk at length about whatever subject you're an expert in. Your passion and experience are where you bring unique value. So don't sweat the writing if you're stuck. Let the people who are trained to help step in and get you past that bump.

Once you've decided to bring in some help during the writing process, there are several ways to move forward. Choosing the right expert can make your book both faster to write and easier to read. If you have the expertise and the message but hesitate at the sight of a blank page, here are some ways editors can help.

Get your ideas on paper

If you're comfortable writing and can get your ideas down fairly quickly, take a few weeks and jot down everything you want to say in your book. The structure doesn't matter so much at this point; what's important is getting your message on paper (or hard drive).

After you have a rough draft, an editor can walk you through what's called a *developmental edit*. The editor will help you arrange your ideas into cohesive chapters, with smoothly flowing ideas and clear takeaways for your readers. Collaborating early will help you avoid any structural problems, ensuring that you address your readers' pain points clearly.

Get a writing coach

If you have a few hours a week to write but don't know how to structure your time—or even where to begin—an editor can direct you through the writing process. This is often called *writing coaching* or *manuscript development*.

An editor can help you refine your approach by discussing your goals for the book and your intended message and then helping you create a detailed outline. If your outline is explicit enough, you can plan out what you want to say in each chapter—and possibly each paragraph in each section of each chapter—before you even begin writing. Then you fill in the blanks to complete your manuscript.

During this level of editing work, your editor will give you manageable writing assignments and will review everything you write to ensure that it stays on topic, clearly expresses your point, and reads well.

Don't be afraid to use a ghostwriter

With the help of a great ghostwriter, the book-writing process can make you a stronger thought leader—and possibly a saner one.

Writing a book is a dream for some business leaders, but it can be a nightmare for others. Those who aren't writers pale at the thought of writing 500 words, let alone 60,000. Unfortunately, this dread of writing holds them back from a multitude of opportunities for exposure and new business.

If you're a non-writer, the good news is that you may be a perfect candidate to enlist the help of a ghostwriter. Like the manuscript development process, ghostwriting starts with discussing your ideas. You'll collaborate with your ghost to determine your message, your audience, and even the tone and voice you want to convey. You'll review the book as it progresses, making sure you and the ghostwriter are still on the same page—pun intended—and the book is shaping up as you'd hoped. Here are a couple of benefits to consider.

WORKING SMARTER, NOT HARDER

Before you ask, the answer is no; ghostwriting isn't cheating, nor is it a sign of laziness. On the contrary, knowing how to delegate is a sign of leadership. Stacy Ennis, ghostwriter and author of *The Editor's Eye*, explains why ghostwriting can be the wisest option to preserve valuable time and resources.

"I like to think of it like this," Ennis says. "I have no interest or skill in accounting, and it's not a good use of my time to study for my CPA. Instead, I pay someone who is an expert in the field (my accountant). My clients are smart, driven, busy people who would rather collaboratively write their books than spend years developing their writing skills."

The heart of writing a book lies in the meat of the idea and the framework that supports it. That can only come from you. The person who puts it down onto paper channels your knowledge.

If I had an electrical issue in my house, I would never dream of trying to fix it myself, given my complete lack of training or understanding of electrical systems. The same is true for ghostwriting. If you have no training in, or understanding of, how to develop an outstanding manuscript, don't try to teach yourself at the expense of your own project. Bring in the help you need.

If you're unsure about working with a ghostwriter, spend some time dissecting your schedule. If you legitimately have every day filled to capacity, or you can list several business-related activities you'd rather spend your time on than writing, it will be worth your time to reach out to a few ghostwriters.

THINKING BIG

If you do decide to enlist the help of a ghostwriter, your experience will be what you make of it. With the help of a ghostwriter who connects well with you, the writing process can be an experience that challenges you in the best way and makes you a stronger thought leader.

"Don't lose sight of the big picture," Ennis says. "Be sure to work with a ghostwriter who gets the larger vision of your brand and understands your long-term goals as an author or influencer. A ghostwriter should be able to help you think strategically about how to approach the book project in relation to overarching strategy, which brings with it the bonus of clarifying other aspects of your work. She should ask a lot of questions and contribute her own thinking and ideas. In essence, look for a ghostwriter who is a thought partner, helping push you to excellence. Not only will this type of person help you write a better book, but the process will be a lot more enriching."

Finding the right ghostwriter is obviously of critical importance. You're looking for someone who has some expertise in your area, shows a commitment to capturing your voice instead of plugging in their own, and has a genuinely inquisitive mind around your subject area. This person will be spending a lot of time interviewing you and asking for your feedback on their work, so fit is paramount. Most ghostwriters will write a sample chapter for you for a fee; this is a worthwhile investment to find the perfect ghost to capture your idea on paper.

If you're planning on using your book to grow your business, a ghostwriter who understands your big-picture goals can also help you keep the content of the book aligned with your brand, creating opportunities for new potential clients to connect with you through your writing.

Writing a book is never a small task, but a skilled ghostwriter who captures your unique perspective can help make the process enriching and beneficial to you and your brand while saving you time and frustration.

Make the creative process work for you

Writing doesn't have to be an insurmountable task. Build scaffolding to support your work, and hire the right people to help you through the rough spots. Your creative mojo will certainly be directed toward creating new content. Regardless, if you have existing content that you think might fit but are unsure how to work in, run it by an editor before dismissing it. And if the whole writing process is overwhelming but you remain passionate about developing a book and doing the extroverted work of hustling publicity and sales (also not an unusual scenario), don't think twice about hiring a manuscript coach or ghostwriter.

Again, it's not unlike any product or business launch. Work your strengths and bring in expert help aligned with your vision for the rest of it. That is not an unusual or lazy way to write. It's smart and efficient.

Chapter 5

THE ACT OF WRITING

Start writing, no matter what. The water does not flow
until the faucet is turned on.
—Louis L'Amour

NOW THAT WE'VE DONE ALL OF THE PREP WORK, let's get to the actual writing. You'll need to think about how you'll tackle the process and how you'll tackle the content.

The process of writing looks different for everyone. There are plenty of frameworks, courses, and conferences designed to help you complete your book, but the fundamentals of developing strong content don't change much. Your writing process may look quite different from another author's process, but you both will cover the same groundwork as you plod toward the finish line.

IS AN OUTLINE OUT OF LINE?

The most basic starting point for writing a book is a well-developed outline. Some writers create outlines just as we were taught in school: in a Word document with major topics, supporting points, conclusions, and so on. Others prefer a more visual approach, using index cards spread on a table or taped to a wall. It really doesn't matter what kind of creative process you use to develop your outline, so don't get too hung up on trying to do it the right way—there's no such thing. You should do whatever works for you.

It's important to note that the outline is basically the blueprint of your book, and as such, it warrants an editor's review before you begin fleshing it out into a full manuscript. Sharing your book at the outline stage gives your editor the chance to identify structural issues, repetition, contradiction, and areas where your content is missing a key concept. Once you and your editor agree on the outline, then you can begin building your manuscript without having to worry about needing to restructure your content later.

Start by organizing your thoughts and fine-tuning your message. Pull your ideas together, and identify your key message, subtopics, talking points, and supporting evidence.

Let's start with your key message. What is the big idea you want someone to take away from your book? Is it to eat healthier, be more frugal, become more organized, or some other idea? Your key message is the end goal and the umbrella under which all of your efforts will fall. For example, let's say you are a physician specializing in integrated medicine—your key message might be something like "treating the whole person and not just the symptoms" or "complete wellness."

Next, brainstorm possible subtopics. Subtopics are the next level in the outline under which you will organize the information, strategies, and tips you will share to help achieve your key message. Often these are represented as chapter or section headings. Using the integrated medicine example above, under the key message "complete wellness," we can establish the following subtopics:

1. Pitfalls of traditional medicine

2. Overview of alternative medicine

3. Integrating traditional and alternative medicine

4. Listening to your body

5. Achieving total wellness

After your subtopics are established, list the talking points that you will discuss under each subheading. Examples, case studies, strategies, and other evidence support the talking points. After the subtopics are established, using our outline above, we will fill out the talking points for the first subtopic:

1. Pitfalls of Traditional Medicine

- Band-Aid Solutions: Focus on symptoms rather than the cause
- Overmedicated: Pros and cons of modern pharmaceuticals
  - Statistics on the number of medicines on the market
  - Statistics on the number of lawsuits or claims from side effects
  - Numbers on the reduction of serious diseases through vaccines and monitored treatment
- Increasing Expense: Rising cost of healthcare
  - Prevention over treatment

As you can see, we have already started to form an outline. This outline is what you will use to create the book proposal, which will also be used to develop the book. Be sure to include statistics, anecdotes, graphs, case studies, and other important information that will help support your points, as these items are key selling points for your proposal and will be important for the publisher to review in the early stages of considering your book for publication.

MAKE IT ACTIONABLE

Content, like fashion, is impacted by trends and culture. While the fundamentals of good content don't waiver much, the ideal tone or presentation of a message will evolve along with the tastes of its audience.

Podcasts, infographics, and the explosive growth of video are popular examples of content *delivery* trends that have risen in recent years. Content *tone* trends can be more difficult to spot.

Running a publishing company with a roster of authors that includes many professional speakers opens up a window to watch trends in both the retail book market and the speaking circuit.

Over the past few years, the content trend that has practically become a mandate is "make it actionable." This is especially true for business books but applies to any nonfiction content intended to help someone develop on a personal or professional level.

Here are four ways to make your content actionable.

Teach, don't tell

Giving your readers the *what* to do is just the starting point. "Engage your audience!" "Upsell more product!" "Give millennials a sense of purpose!" All of these are examples of *what* that require clearly defined next steps in order to actually be useful.

Rise above basic, surface-level content and give clear guidance and action steps like checklists, frameworks, reading resources, and exercises for the reader to implement so that they're not left guessing at how to get to the result you're prescribing. When you give your reader the tools to put your recommendations to work, you're creating real value.

Some authors cringe at the notion of "giving away the farm," especially if they are consultants who use a framework to solve problems for their clients. Remember that the DIY audience was never going to hire you in the first place. Your real audience appreciates the experience you bring to your area of knowledge, and giving them a taste of your approach is more likely to prequalify compatible clients than drive them away.

Naturally, this can't be applied to all content (editorial opinion pieces, for instance), but for most prescriptive nonfiction, this is a requirement whether the content falls into book form, video, blog, podcast, or another format.

Emphasize the learning elements

Providing a set of tools for your reader to use is a differentiator and a selling point, and it should be highlighted visually and through the organization of the content.

Use call-out boxes to distinguish action items within your content, and make it easy for the reader to act on your advice. Using a consistent design theme to identify these tools will help organize your content and empower the reader to easily pursue (and reference) next steps.

Consistent themes also work well to cue the reader when you're giving them action items. For example, Beth Levine's communication skills book, *Jock Talk*, incorporates consistent action items at the end of each chapter. In this case, they are simply takeaway tips (a summary of the main learning points) and exercises (self-explanatory). Some authors brand these action items to tie them back to the larger framework they teach.

Use stories and examples

Given that your readers will be bringing their own worldviews to how they view your content, it's important to provide stories and examples to illustrate your ideas and help the reader visualize your advice in action. Stories, metaphors, and examples make ideas memorable and relatable.

New York Times best-selling authors Chip and Dan Heath do an excellent job of using stories and metaphors to drive home the frameworks in their books, and then of using those stories as reminder prompts within the takeaway action framework. I encourage you to pick up any of their books and take a look to see what I'm talking about.

Highlight your team

Whether you're the CEO writing articles about how your company succeeds or you're a content writer in charge of your company's blog, it's quite possible that you know a lot of the *what* to do without being knee-deep in the *how* to do it.

For that reason, developing actionable content provides a great opportunity to highlight the deep subject area expertise of your team. You can structure this type of content in an interview or Q&A format, or you can split it up between an introduction of the *what* from one person followed by the *how* from another. (Be sure to play up that person's expertise and credentials to get the reader excited for the transition.)

Allowing your company's staff to step up and share their knowledge helps ensure strong, actionable content in addition to publicly recognizing them for their subject expertise.

As you're planning next year's content strategy, deliberately design your writing to be actionable using the tips in this section. Your readers will appreciate the meaningful content and will therefore be more likely to share your work with others, multiplying the fruits of your labor.

SCHEDULING TIME

Writers groups and accountability partners are great if you have trouble summoning up the will to write. But for nonfiction writers who are often running businesses, working demanding jobs, traveling for gigs as consultants or speakers, and so on, the primary issue is often one of time, not of will. Given all of the demands of our day jobs, plus the inevitable demands of our personal life and a few blessed hours for unwinding or hobbies, you may be wondering how it's mathematically possible to produce a finished manuscript within a reasonable timeframe.

Speaking of math, let's break it down. A typical 200-page manuscript is roughly 60,000 words. (Pro tip: For a typical nonfiction book with minimal pictures or illustrations, word count divided by 300 will give you a rough idea of the number of pages you'll have in your final book.)

You may be wondering why the publishing world is so hung up on reaching a length of 200 pages. Many of the authors I work with make the valid point that, increasingly, readers take in shorter-form content and therefore may not want to read something so long. After all, we don't want to create a book that is 50 pages of excellent content and 150 pages of fluff.

The reason the 200 page count holds up as a benchmark of sorts has to do with merchandising and price modeling in the brick-and-mortar retail world. A book that is shorter than 200 pages ends up with a thin spine, which becomes lost on a bookstore shelf. Retailers also make their purchases based in part on their historical data related to how titles of a similar subject, length, and price point performed. From the retail buyer's perspective, in most cases a twenty-dollar product should probably be close to 200 pages. In the interest of maximizing chances for retail performance, all of these factors play into that 200-page goal.

If you're sitting in front of what you thought was a robust 2,000-word outline, I understand how overwhelmed you must be feeling right now. But writing 60,000 words is entirely doable if you apply some discipline to the process. This may also serve as a good reality check about the time you need to dedicate to complete your manuscript on the timeline you're hoping to achieve.

As a point of reference, a typical nonfiction advice article for a mainstream business site is about 700 words. Assuming those 2,000 words in your outline all need to be replaced with content, you'll need to write roughly eighty-five article-length chunks to flesh out a book. Write one 700-word chunk a day, five days a week, and you'll be done with your manuscript in just over four months.

FOUR MONTHS! That's forever! This is what you're thinking, isn't it? Let's unpack this deal—four months of a 700-word daily commitment for the payoff of bringing your life's work to paper to inspire others, to drive change, and to make a difference that will carry your brand and your work for years to come. Four months and you have the heavy lifting of writing a book behind you. Four months between being an author and not being an author. Four months will pass in the blink of an eye. It's up to you to put a system in place to capitalize on it and get the writing wheels in motion.

Here are five tips to help you knock out those 700 words a day.

Calendar it

For most of us, what looks like a clear, prime-for-writing day on the calendar can quickly turn into a day of putting out fires and generally being drawn into competing demands that take us away from our writing goals.

If you've committed to 700 words a day, you are serious about finishing your book. With that being the case, you need to schedule time for writing on your calendar and not let anything outside of a legit emergency come between you and your standing meeting with your manuscript. This is a priority. Don't let anyone convince you that finishing a book is a pipe dream that can wait for later. Stick to your guns, and do the work. Add the recurring meeting with yourself to your calendar so nobody can book time with you during your writing slot. Honor that commitment, and don't break it for anything that can wait.

You may be thinking, "Okay, I'll condense the fifteen minutes a day I had planned for writing into roughly one hour a week." Don't practice false efficiency. For all but the most experienced writers, the regular practice of writing for fifteen minutes a day will be much more effective at creating a habit of getting words onto paper than one session of attempted writing for one hour a week. What if your weekly hour of writing time is interrupted/taken away or entirely unproductive? To make meaningful progress on your manuscript, you need to carve out a more regular window of uninterrupted work time.

Get comfortable

Sometimes, immersing yourself in an environment conducive to getting your creative juices flowing makes the difference between one hour spent staring at a blank screen and one hour spent churning out 700 precious words.

Sitting at your office desk and trying to write will most likely be a challenge. Despite your best efforts to do otherwise, you will almost instinctively be checking email, listening to hallway conversations, and breaking concentration at the sound of a ringing phone. Don't feel weak for this; it's a behavior pattern that you've been grooming for years.

To knock out a consistent 700 words a day, you may need your own writing sanctuary. Whether the writing muse visits you most frequently in a coffee shop, in a local park, or at home, that's the place you should plan to be each time you expect yourself to write. This will help snap your brain into writing mode and help you postpone the many distractions that can otherwise stand between you and your writing goals.

Set a goal

Speaking of goals, it's helpful to give yourself a concrete target to hit each time you write. Whether it's 700 words, 500 words, or simply fifteen minutes of constant writing without regard for word count, knowing what you need to accomplish when you sit down to write will help you move through the task at hand.

Let it flow

It's easy to get overwhelmed by the idea of writing something that will eventually be published for all to read (and review). Publishing a book is a very vulnerable experience. The good news is that your team of experts will help you polish that manuscript later. For now, just get words onto the page without getting hung up on grammar, syntax, and the like.

It's also helpful to carry a notebook (or use the notes or memo recording app on your phone) to capture flashes of inspiration to incorporate into your writing later. Don't trust yourself to remember it; write it down!

Find a partner

Having an accountability partner is a great way to keep your writing efforts on track. Perhaps this person is also writing a book, or perhaps it's a colleague or trusted friend who won't be afraid to push you to stick to your commitment.

This person can simply check in with you a few times a week to ask how your writing for the week has been going or what you're planning on working on in your next writing session. Honor this person's commitment to help you succeed, and do your part to be ready for their check-ins.

These tips should help you successfully complete that manuscript. Above all, remember that this writing grind is temporary. Imagine the sense of accomplishment you'll feel once you put the proverbial pencil down and can say your manuscript is done and the sense of pride you'll have when you can say, "Yes, I wrote a book!"

Structure is key

Structure is the key to writing a good book. I mean that in two ways: Structuring the book allows you to create coherent content in less time and with reduced effort for both you (in writing it) and your reader (in reading it). Structuring your writing process helps you get through what is otherwise the nightmare of blank pages staring back at you while you face a looming deadline to write a set amount each day.

If you find yourself stuck, take the time to analyze that situation so you better understand the roadblock. Is your outline too specific, creating a forced structure that limits your writing flow? Or is it too general, making it difficult to decide on what to include and what to exclude?

There's no shame in revising and reworking the process that best suits you. Just don't stop writing. It's hard to pick momentum back up once you've stopped, and launching your big idea will require all the momentum.

Chapter 6

PROTECTING YOUR CONTENT

*Only one thing is impossible for God: to find any sense
in any copyright law on the planet.*
—Mark Twain

YOUR BOOK IS THE CULMINATION OF YOUR IDEAS, your experiences, your insights, and a ton of hard work, so it's important that this intellectual property is protected from infringement and other threats. Imitation is perhaps the sincerest form of flattery, but flattery is no comfort if someone else starts profiting from material that you created. You can best protect yourself with a basic understanding of copyrights, trademarks, and subsidiary rights and the ways they apply to your book. Even if your publisher is in charge of protecting your work, it's wise to ask educated questions and review everything you sign with an attorney who specializes in intellectual property law.

COPYRIGHT PROTECTION FOR AUTHORS

First things first, let's establish a basic understanding of copyright related to published works. A copyright is the exclusive right to print or publish your material and to authorize others to do the same. Copyrights are also useful to authors because their power stretches into TV, film, and other industries where the book could be used without permission. Copyrights do not cover your ideas in and of themselves but, rather, the unique expression of them. The term *unique* is important; without it, someone could conceivably write one book about how to lead a successful sales team and shut the whole genre down.

A copyright technically goes into effect the moment your content is created, but in order to legally enforce the copyright, it's still necessary to register with the US Copyright Office. If you're working with a publisher, they'll typically take care of the registration as a matter of routine, but it's still wise to make sure that is addressed in your agreement and to obtain documentation when it is complete.

Before registering a copyright, you need to make sure you are not in violation of any other copyrights. If you use song lyrics, images, or excerpts of other works in your book, you could be at risk for being sued for copyright infringement if you have not been given permission from the owner. Some uses (parody, critique, research) can be categorized as *fair use* and may not require permission, but that depends on how much content you borrowed and other factors, which, unfortunately, can only be weighed and clearly assessed by a court. This makes it important to have your licenses in order or, if you do decide that you want to rely on fair use, to consult early and often with an intellectual property attorney.

Public domain

In terms of using outside works in your book, the only relatively safe area is true public domain works, which means books published before 1923 and government works. I say *relatively* because there are sometimes exceptions to the exceptions, so again, if you are not absolutely sure whether something is public domain (and content being readily available on the Internet does not automatically qualify), you should review it with your attorney.

What you can trademark and what you cannot

A trademark is a symbol, word, or words legally registered or established by use as representing a company or product. Though trademarks also protect intellectual property, the requirements to register a trademark are more stringent than those for copyrights. This can strengthen the protection around the expression of your ideas.

The chances of your trademark registration being approved are dependent on your intentions and some factors from the outside world. For example, if disruption is a theme in your book, you can't trademark the word *disruption* unless it is connected to a good or service that you're selling. Common words are also difficult to trademark, because of the likelihood that the trademark would be violated every day. That said, if you wanted to trademark "John Smith's Disruptive Method for Success," a tutorial that you sell to your clients, you would stand a much better chance of having your trademark approved. You could also trademark the title of a series, like *The John Smith Disruptive Method for Success* series, because it is a unique title for a product that you're selling.

Additionally, keep in mind that the trademark will apply only within your specific market and class of services. A trademark registration can be particularly advantageous if you're the first in your industry to trademark the title of an important service, but difficulties can arise if you've trademarked the title of your book series, but someone is trying to claim film or TV rights to your work through copyright through a publishing agreement. Before you attempt to register a trademark, conduct thorough research on what you're trying to trademark and its competition so you can assess whether it makes sense to seek a registration. If you're not sure, here are a few questions to help you get started:

- Is this mark directly related to my product or service?
- Is this mark commonly used in my industry or by the general population?
- Is anyone else already using this, and if so, do they already have it trademarked or have a significant brand presence anywhere that could lead to confusion in the marketplace?

So let's say that you have done your initial analysis. We'll assume you answer yes to the first question above and no to the other two questions. It is looking like our *The John Smith Disruptive Method for Success* mark could be used to build out your brand and platform. If you went with a traditional publisher for your book, there is another question for you and your attorney to consider—and preferably consider before you incur all of the legal search fees that go with a trademark application process:

What rights to the title did I grant or assign to the publisher?

Many authors are surprised that even though they may have come up with their own title and made their intended uses for it in their business platform clear to their publisher contractually, the publisher may have taken some rights to the title. Depending on the terms of the agreement, this could prevent the author from using the title in their business.

This is not a hypothetical scenario. I have worked with authors who have found themselves in this predicament with their traditional publisher and who then pivoted to the hybrid publishing model in order to retain those rights and fully use them for their business platforms. If you are starting a new business using your book content or book title as a pillar for your services and platform, this is a very important item to keep in mind when considering your publishing options and in negotiating any deals with traditional publishers.

WHO OWNS YOUR WORK?

Now that we've gone over the basics of the copyright and trademark processes, the next question that usually comes up is who handles the copyright filing—the publisher or the author?

The answer depends on your agreement with the publisher.

In the traditional publishing model, the publisher would likely take care of the copyright filing.

On the opposite end of the spectrum, authors who opt to self-publish their books maintain all the rights to their work and bear the burden of protecting that work on their own.

Hybrid publishers can go either way. Greenleaf Book Group, for example, allows authors to maintain all intellectual property rights to their content but offers to handle the copyright filing on their behalf.

Owning the copyright of your work also gives you control over infringement actions, including Internet takedown requests under the Digital Millennium Copyright Act (DMCA) to prevent infringement of your work. This comes into play in the rare case when an unauthorized person posts portions (or all) of your book online without your permission or lifts your content completely and posts it with a title and cover of their own creation.

If you have a coauthor or contributor to your work, you should get a written assignment of all copyrights and make sure any contributed content from those contributors is either original or has the proper permissions or licenses to be used in your book. This basically means that your contributor will be providing content on a work-for-hire basis, assigning the copyright on their material to you.

In any case, even a traditional publisher doesn't technically take all rights. You always retain copyright, unless you sold it in a work-for-hire arrangement, which transfers copyright away from you.

Ownership of rights can be tricky on the legal side. For many authors, the question of who owns their work can be a deal breaker, especially when it comes to subsidiary rights.

WHAT ARE SUBSIDIARY RIGHTS?

When thinking about your book's rights, it's best to think of that protection as a collection of smaller rights. While you can sign over most rights to a traditional publisher, in many cases, there is room to negotiate exactly which rights they receive.

This leads us to subsidiary rights, which are most easily defined as the rights to produce different versions of the book outside of the original publication format. A few examples of subsidiary rights include—

- **Reprint Rights:** This includes publishing versions of your book in paperback, large format, illustrated format, braille, and so on.

- **Film Rights:** If a producer wants to make a movie or television series based on a book, they will negotiate the terms with the holder of the film rights.

- **Book Club Rights:** Book clubs, like Book of the Month, may negotiate special deals or printings with the copyright holder.
- **Audio Rights:** This includes the rights to produce and distribute an audiobook version of the work.
- **Translation Rights:** Foreign publishers may contact the rights owner to create and distribute a version of the book that has been translated into another language.

At first glance, it might seem much simpler to sign over all of these rights to the publisher and let them negotiate on your behalf. After all, they have strong connections within the industry and more knowledge around terms. What could be the downside?

The best way to answer that question is to have an honest assessment of your goals for the book. For many authors, the book is part of a much larger business or initiative, and their goals don't stop at book sales.

If you intend to use your book to bolster your company or brand, subsidiary rights dealing with ancillary products may be extremely important to maintain. For instance, without the proper subsidiary rights, you may be limited in your ability to produce things like online courses, workshops, or speeches that rely on your content.

Understanding how you would like to use your content in the future will help guide your decisions about how to publish your work and which rights to grant.

Should you go the traditional publishing route, you also do not want to be in a position where the publisher ties up your work and loses interest in supporting it. The publisher converting the book to print-on-demand status in order to keep it on their list without any associated overhead from printing inventory usually indicates this swing. Print-on-demand distribution can limit brick-and-mortar retail access, so if this is a concern, confirm that your agreement includes a *reversion of rights* set of terms that outlines the scenarios (switching to digital distribution via print-on-demand, abandonment during the production process, etc.) where you are able to reclaim your rights and take back control of your work.

A CLOSER LOOK AT FOREIGN RIGHTS, OR TRANSLATION RIGHTS

What do Dan Brown and Pope Benedict have in common? Not much, but they do both know how to take advantage of translation rights, a sector of the publishing industry where the right book and the right deal can provide a nice padding of revenue for authors and publishers.

Dan Brown's cultural juggernaut, *The Da Vinci Code*, was translated into well over forty languages, doing particularly well in Europe, where publishers obtained rights to the ubiquitous book and watched it top bestseller lists for months.

And the Pope? His Italian publisher, Rizzoli, sold North American rights to his *Jesus of Nazareth* to Doubleday, which was a Random House imprint. Doubleday not only bought the English rights to the book in North America but wisely snapped up Spanish-language rights as well— due, of course, to the vast population of Spanish-speaking Catholics on the continent.

These deals show how the rights to best-selling books travel globally, but even without bestseller status, many nonfiction authors have found that selling translation rights to their books creates a nice way to diversify and expand revenue with no upfront cost.

Some publishers will manage this process as an area of rights that they hold. If you retain translation rights, you can enlist the help of an agent to solely chase down translation rights deals. Naturally, an agent will only want to spend time on titles with real potential in this market.

As you consider whether your book has the potential for overseas translation, here are some points to remember.

Your book must travel well

Keep in mind that content must be relevant to appeal to foreign publishers and agents. Books that hit the big time in foreign markets must have somewhat universal subject matter, and it helps if they are easily translated as well; the prospect of spending valuable time and money on a long and difficult translation can kill off agents' and publishers' interest in no time. Popular categories tend to be business, self-help, parenting, and personal empowerment. Fiction is likely to do well only if it has a stellar track record of sales and broad appeal.

Depending on the publisher and how the work translates, changes in format may occur during this process. A slim book may fatten considerably in certain languages. Your trim size may change. Pictures and illustrations you don't have the right to sell may have to be removed. And don't leave any ugly messages on your Israeli publisher's voicemail for printing your book backwards—it's supposed to be like that.

The price must be right

Hammering out the royalties and advance terms with a foreign publisher can be tricky, particularly when dealing with exchange rates and cross-cultural bargaining. Royalty rates are typically between 5 and 10 percent. A couple of seasoned foreign rights negotiators suggest using the following formula to come up with a rough idea of a reasonable advance:

$$[\textbf{anticipated first print run}] \times [\textbf{royalty percentage}] \times [\textbf{retail price}] = [\textbf{your advance}]$$

Translation rights grants generally last around four to five years, and royalties can be paid anywhere from every six months to annually. But just like traditional publishing deals in the United States, it's unusual to see much money beyond the advance paid on your translation rights.

Terms must be defined

Make sure you know exactly what you sold and for how long. Are audio rights and book club rights included in the deal? Are you selling the right to distribute your book in Spain or anywhere they speak Spanish? Clearing up issues like these can help you sidestep future issues and get the most out of your translation agreement.

Communication must be sustained

Your involvement in the translation process will be minimal, if you're involved at all, so don't be surprised if you don't hear from the foreign publisher during the production process. Without being overly pushy, try to check in with these contacts and maintain a healthy relationship.

Great distances can create great frustration when the lines go dead for long periods of time. Many newbies to foreign distribution tell horror stories of backed-up royalties and unresponsive contacts.

Longtime foreign rights negotiators emphasize that personal relationships are often vital in a successful deal. Your contacts should, for the most part, speak English, but cultural differences remain. Naturally, remember to be polite, friendly, and respectful, and studying up on the country in question doesn't hurt either. Embarrassing geography gaffes or a bad attitude could easily prompt a publisher to pass you over for another of the many titles ripe for successful foreign sales. Ultimately, it's not likely that the translation rights to your book will pave your road to riches. It may seem a daunting task for a modest amount of money, but anything you make is basically found money. (It's also fun to tell your friends that your book is big in Latvia.)

Foreign readers are hungry for quality books. If yours fits the bill, send it packing and see what happens.

Protect your intellectual property

Copyright law isn't fun, but it's important to understand its implications on the publishing path that you choose. Think about the words *intellectual property*. We're dealing with the end product of your lifetime of experience, wisdom, emotional investment, and, yes, intellect. Your intellectual property is an extraordinarily valuable resource that should be protected and managed in a way that allows you to reap maximum benefit from the years it took you to develop, create, and document it. Whether that means choosing a publishing model that supports your ownership of rights or negotiating like a champ to carve out rights that your publisher can't exploit, take a strong stance on the equity you've earned around your idea.

Once you know which rights you can manage, work them into your overall launch plan so they don't sit on the back burner and fall victim to missed opportunities. If you are maintaining control of your rights, you are also the boss and steward of those rights and how they are managed. When interest picks up around your book via media profiles, bestseller lists, "best of" features, and so on, you will need to be ready to jump on the opportunity to pitch foreign rights deals, movie options, and the like.

If you're handling this on your own, prepare in advance using resources and partners like the Copyright Clearance Center to ensure that you have connections in place and are ready to strike when the iron is hot. Quite often, opportunities beget more opportunities.

PART 2

INFLUENCE

Chapter 7

BUILDING A PLATFORM

With public sentiment, nothing can fail. Without it, nothing can succeed.
—Abraham Lincoln

MONEY IS PERSONAL. Spilling your economic guts to anyone other than your spouse, partner, or family members is unheard of for most people—but not for Suze Orman. Orman, a financial advisor turned television host and best-selling author, made a hugely successful career of listening to personal financial pain on a daily basis and giving empowering solutions for people in tough situations. Her advice is often abrasive. She challenges her fans to make immediate, proactive changes in their financial lives that are never easy for anyone to make.

With her in-your-face approach and established expertise, Orman's reach extends to millions of people. Her TV program, *The Suze Orman Show*, enjoyed twelve seasons as one of the most highly rated programs on CNBC. She's also penned nine consecutive bestsellers and hosted the most successful fundraiser in the history of PBS. That's powerful.

Everyone wants Suze's advice. And when Suze talks, not only do people listen but they also share what they've heard with others. She gets people talking, which helps drive word of mouth. It's hard not to admire Suze's ability to wield widespread influence and connect so strongly with an audience in this subject area. Orman's path to platform success is worthy of study. It didn't happen overnight, but she tapped into a deep need (personal financial advice) and transformed that into a brand—one that captured people's attention.

If ideas are your foundation when it comes to building a successful platform, influence is your most important tool. Without meaningful influence, great ideas can die. So find your audience, cultivate your relationships through offline and online channels, and build a following. Will you become a best-selling author like Suze Orman? If publishers had a crystal ball, they'd only publish the sure bets. But you can maximize your chances by taking your platform building seriously.

Every author wants to write a bestseller. For some, it's a stretch goal. For others, it's a business strategy. Being able to call yourself a best-selling author (as long as it's on a legitimate print list like *The New York Times* or *The Wall Street Journal*) can be a big credibility booster and can even warrant increased speaking fees. An active, engaged base of readers is a crucial part of attaining that goal, so when authors tell me they want to become Greenleaf Book Group's next best-selling author, we turn our attention to ensuring that their platform is abundant, aligned, and advocating on their behalf. We'll call that list of features our *A-list*, and these attributes are not limited to the publishing realm: What helps to sell an author's books is not far removed from what helps to sell any company's product.

In publishing, we use the word *platform* to refer to the group of people an author can realistically reach who identify as part of that author's community. They are supporters, tribe members. They have bought into the author's message and want more. A platform is not just a brand. It starts with a brand, but it is really composed of an engaged audience. These are the raving fans that every business wants. Just like a physical stage, your platform of readers serves to elevate. In this sense, it's elevating you and your message over the crowd.

For any book, the content itself is (and will always be) vitally important to its long-term success. It needs to fill a need or be entertaining. Long-term sales are an important goal, but becoming a best-selling author requires velocity of sales since print lists are calculated weekly. To move thousands of books in a one-week period, an author needs to campaign and activate their entire platform to support the launch effort. A bestseller doesn't have to happen in week one of release, but for multiple reasons oriented around building momentum through retail networks, that first week is ideal. Retailers are trained to respond to trends, and if you can show your book is trending as a new release, you can leverage that for widened distribution.

Abundance

Returning to our A-list, exactly how much abundance do you need? It's different for every author, and it depends on your track record for converting your audience into customers. Just remember that your word-of-mouth sales will typically come after the initial launch period; people need time to read the book. If you want to pile thousands of sales into week one, it follows that you'll need to directly hustle thousands of people to order from within your own platform.

Alignment

An abundant platform is important, but it's not a guarantee of book sales in and of itself. To leverage an abundant platform, your product needs to be aligned with your brand. By way of example, consider *Rebels: City of Indra* from Kylie and Kendall Jenner. These two share a combined Instagram following of over 110 million. That's a number just 18 million shy of the entire population of Mexico. Yet as of June 2017, *Rebels* had reportedly sold just under 17,000 copies since its release in June of 2014.[1] Why? It's easy to question the validity of their social media followers, but even if we boldly assume half of those accounts are fake, the release-to-date sales still demonstrate a horrible conversion rate. The real issue is that this product does not align with what Kendall and Kylie's platform wants. Their audience wants lip kits, fashion, and celebrities—not a dystopian girl-power tale of "air, fire, and a bond of blood." There's nothing

---

1   Daniel Barna, "Surprise! Kendall & Kylie Jenner's Book Is a Major Flop," Refinery29, October 30, 2014, http://www.refinery29.com/2014/10/77080/kendall-kylie-jenner-rebels-of-indra-flop.

wrong with that topic; it's just not aligned with the authors' platform. The Jenner sisters would be more successful in publishing if they were mindful of their own brand and audience demographics.

The takeaway here is that alignment is critical, and as tempting as it can be to stray from a core brand to grab any available dollar, it's imperative to say no to misaligned opportunities.

Advocacy

Finally, a powerful platform advocates. There is no marketing tool more powerful than the enthusiastic recommendation of a happy customer. Networking, word-of-mouth marketing, social proof, reviews, and all other ways of generally influencing peers hold the proverbial keys to the kingdom of long-term sales. If you honor your audience and deliver a quality product, they will reward you with the multiplying power of their recommendations. That will certainly make future bestseller launches easier!

Fundamentally, a book is a consumer product. As we well know in our industry, having a standout product is not enough to make it successful. Book sales are predominantly author driven. According to Verso Digital's 2009 Survey of Book-Buying Behavior, author reputation is the most important factor in a book purchase decision, followed by personal recommendation and price. This is why we hear so much talk about author platform. Your platform is your brand power, and while some are happy accidents, most are quite carefully planned. The good news is that any author can lay the groundwork for a strategically built platform.

The first rule of generating word-of-mouth buzz is to give people something to talk about. A book launch gives you the opportunity to launch a media campaign around your book's release, a reason for you to connect with the media as an expert source, and a physical tool to deliver to reporters, meeting planners who might be interested in you as a speaker, and your internal list of past and prospective clients. All of these lend power to your author platform. But even before your launch, you can start building your platform. The crucial elements of platform building are planning, evaluating your current platform and brand, and being consistent and authentic with your audience.

BUILD YOUR PLATFORM EARLY

Not only is your platform crucial but you must begin building it early. Seriously, you should start *right now*.

It comes down to a fundamental truth in the media world: We have a huge supply of and a limited demand for content. Consider the person you are trying to reach with your message. This person's attention is spread very thin as a result of life in general, just like you. Reading time is limited, so he or she will choose carefully. Never mind that hundreds of thousands of books are published every year; your reader is also being courted by bloggers, television, magazines, YouTube, Netflix, and on and on. Add in the fact that reading a book is a bigger time commitment than most other media, and you will quickly realize that when you ask someone to buy your book, you are not only asking them for twenty dollars; you're also asking them for two weeks of their time.

Entrepreneur Gary Vaynerchuk has appeared on programs ranging from *Ellen* to NPR to CNN. He's written a *New York Times* and *Wall Street Journal* bestseller and has well over one million Twitter followers. He grew his family wine business from revenues of $3 million per year to over $45 million in eight short years. By the time Vaynerchuk was just thirty-five years old, he operated a slew of businesses and could boast a gaggle of fans that referred to themselves as *Vayniacks*. In short, he was a walking billboard of what a concentrated platform can do for you if you build it before your launch.

BUILD YOUR PLATFORM WELL

But where do you begin a task as daunting as becoming a veritable expert like Vaynerchuk? A strong platform starts with your ideas. Your ideas are your foundation; they're what you offer your audience, and they're what will make you money.

Building valuable content that an audience will care about and pay to access depends on many factors, including finding your passion, identifying your audience and its needs, and connecting that passion to that audience with appropriate content. Let's walk through this process and take a closer look at what this means.

Identify your passion

It is essential that you care about your topic. If you're not engaged, your audience certainly won't be—and you'll probably lose steam under the load of all of this writing and platform-building work. Ideally, you will be passionate in an area where you're already credentialed. If you're a professional magician who wants to create a platform in the world of deep-sea diving, you'll have to work a lot harder than someone who's already in the water.

Connect with your platform

Do you want to create your own content, or is your staff aligned with your message enough to do it for you? Your answer to these questions might depend on whether you're creating a platform for yourself or your business (or whether your "self" is your business). If you are developing your personal platform, it's important that fans feel like they're interacting with the real you—not your personal assistant. As literary agent Rachelle Gardner writes on her blog, "It's harder than ever to attract people to books. The way to do it is increasingly through *personal connection*, and that means *you*, the author, making connections with your readers."[2]

Vaynerchuk took the time each week to record himself on camera for his (now retired) video blog, *The Daily Grape*. He was being himself for his fans. Glancing at his Twitter feed, you'll see that it's a stream of responses to his followers. No wonder people feel connected to him: They *are*.

---

2   Rachelle Gardner, "The Dreaded Author Platform," http://www.rachellegardner.com/the-dreaded-author-platform.

Decide on a content strategy

How will you present your content? Through blogging, videos, presentations, webinars, articles, or a book? A mix of these is likely the most effective way to present your content, but it's important to know what your audience responds to. How do they learn best? And what works for your content? Do that!

Collect and organize

Building your platform requires content, and here's the big tip I'd offer to build strong platform messaging: Don't lose your content! You need every bit of it to redistribute and heighten your platform. Once you have your content arsenal ready to go, there are a number of ways to get the most use out of it. Keep a record of your newsletter tips, blog posts, radio and TV interviews, lecture recordings, and so on. Create your own system to tag your content by subject area to come up with a messaging matrix for easy syndication and so that you'll be able to quickly repurpose your content for requested media pieces, op-eds, and the like. This organized approach to content management will save you many headaches down the road.

Check and double-check that the content matches your audience's needs

Conduct an audience analysis before you begin aggressively interacting with them. Who are they? What do they do? What do they struggle with? What do they care about, and who else do they listen to? Knowing what your competitors bring to the table is essential too. You must differentiate yourself and should focus on filling a hole in the field.

Vaynerchuk had the foresight to realize that e-commerce would grow exponentially and started winelibrary.com in 1997. He also quickly identified an empty spot in the wine-tasting world—non-fluffy, honest feedback. He started making wine review videos and spoke to his audience on their level, using terms like *sniffy sniff* and *oakmonster*. His reviews were soon reaching over 100,000 viewers per day. He filled a need in the lofty world of wine collecting with excellent, informed content in a guy-next-door voice.

Create solid new content on a regular basis

Make a schedule and stick to it. Develop an editorial calendar to keep your content consistent. The Content Marketing Institute provides a guide to starting an editorial calendar, pointing out that the calendar not only keeps you on track but helps you think of ways to repurpose your content as well.[3]

Keeping with the Vaynerchuk example, let's imagine what an editorial calendar might have looked like for him. We'll start by organizing content into general buckets. In this case, that's reds, whites, rosés, and food pairings. We'll plan to post four videos per week, one from each category. Mondays will be for red wine, Tuesdays for white, Thursdays for rosé, and Fridays for food pairing ideas.

Next, break those broad buckets down into different subcategories of content. Within reds, we'll list out different wine varietals (Merlot, Cabernet Sauvignon, Malbec, etc.). You could also opt to break it down by country of origin. Whatever you decide, keep it consistent. You'll want to space these subcategories out so that you don't end up reviewing three kinds of Malbecs within a month, leaving your Merlot lovers without any content.

Now, we'll plan out specific blog posts. Use a calendar tool, like Google Calendar or Basecamp, to schedule these, like in the example on the opposite page.

Mapping out your content like this allows you to visualize it and notice patterns. Keep defaulting to Cabernet Sauvignon posts? Maybe you should do a special episode or a short series on them, or just try to space them out more.

Before your editorial calendar is complete, there are still a few more things to consider. When is each piece due? If you have multiple contributors, who will be completing each assignment? And, specific to this example, exactly which wines will you be discussing each day? Make it as detailed as you can.

---

3   Michele Linn, "How to Put Together an Editorial Calendar for Content Marketing," Content Marketing Institute, August 16, 2010, http://contentmarketinginstitute.com/2010/08/content-marketing-editorial-calendar/.

Monday	Tuesday	Wednesday	Thursday	Friday
Red: Merlot	White: Chardonnay		Rosé: Pinot Noir	Food Pairing: Classic Hamburger
Red: Cabernet Sauvignon	White: Riesling		Rosé: Shiraz	Food Pairing: Takeout Thai Food
Red: Malbec	White: Chenin Blanc		Rosé: Merlot	Food Pairing: Texas BBQ
Red: Pinot Noir	White: Viognier		Rosé: Chardonnay	Food Pairing: Pizza

You should also keep it flexible. The goal is to keep you organized, not to box you in creatively. If you have the opportunity to collaborate with someone influential on a post, do it! And if you feel like your content is getting stale, make adjustments. Look back on past calendars for inspiration and guidance about what resonated with your audience and what didn't. By keeping an editorial calendar, you will be able to stay organized and make the best use of your content, like Vaynerchuk.

Keep up with new developments in your field

Now that you're seen as an expert, you need to remain one. Your audience needs to know they can depend on you for new information and ideas.... Otherwise, you will lose them to the next bright voice in your field.

When passion, good ideas, and your audience's needs work together, great content results. Vaynerchuk took what he knew and loved (wine) and spoke to his audience in a unique and refreshing way (casually) in a medium they responded to (video blogging). Above all, he was (and is) authentic. Putting on airs and writing, speaking, or interviewing in a voice that is not truly yours is exhausting. You will not be able to maintain it long enough to build a solid platform, and it will fall apart in time because you won't care about maintaining your alter ego. Be yourself and search hard for what makes you special. It's what draws others to you.

Vaynerchuk's success all started with his content, and yours will too. The more content you create over time, the more your ideas become the engine that powers your brand platform. After all, they don't say "content is king" for nothing.

EVALUATE YOUR BRAND

In order to effectively build your brand, you need to know your starting point, the current status of your brand. A *brand audit* is a tool that companies use to analyze their brand and marketing effectiveness, to identify forward-looking brand goals, to expose gaps between how the company sees its brand and how consumers see it, and to get everyone on the same proverbial page regarding messaging. Quite a lot goes into a corporate brand audit—brand SWOT (strengths, weaknesses, opportunities, and threats) analysis, business plans, creative briefs, ad materials, press releases, analyst reports, and more. Without going quite that far, as an author, you can benefit from a basic, objective brand audit. Let's take a look at some standard brand audit components that you can use to your advantage.

Brand identity

Brand identity is made up of a number of elements under your control that a consumer may notice and associate with your brand. Some components will be specific to the author while others pertain more to the author's product. Over time, consistent brand identity increases brand awareness. Take inventory of these elements and document them so they can be easily shared with anyone working on your brand.

POSITIONING STATEMENT

What do you offer your reader? You've heard this called *the promise*. It will generally fall under information or entertainment. Maybe you offer actionable tools for small businesses to increase profits fast or compelling science fiction rooted in well-researched facts. Successfully branded writers are strongly differentiated from others in their field and generally stay true to the same basic promise across all works.

TAGLINE

This is usually a very short, memorable phrase that reinforces an important aspect of your brand. It can be descriptive or expressive. For example, CNN's tagline is "The most trusted name in news" (descriptive). Author Daniel Amen's is "The Brain Doctor." McDonald's expressive tagline is "I'm lovin' it." Note that it's easier to pull off an expressive tagline if your brand is already well known.

LOGO

The symbol that identifies your brand is your logo. Think the Nike swoosh or Apple's apple with a bite missing. A publishing company will typically have an imprint logo. An individual author probably does not need to develop a logo. In either case, if you do have a logo, stick with it. Recognition and consistency are key.

TYPESTYLE AND COLORS

In the print world, typestyle and colors can be powerful product-branding tools, especially for a series. Search *Rich Dad, Poor Dad* online and notice the consistent use of purple and gold. The *Twilight* series uses a distinctive typeface and a strong black, white, and red palette.

All these elements and details are important when developing your brand identity. They may seem small, but they are things the reader will come to know and recognize as being distinctly you.

Brand image

While brand identity pertains to who you are, brand image speaks to how you are perceived. You actively develop brand identity, whereas brand image is passive and seen through consumers' eyes. For instance, your website might have language positioning you as a social media or web 2.0 expert . . . but the weak social media profiles, low follower numbers, and dated website design contributing to your image could undermine that identity.

For published authors, reviews and press mentions are an easy way to begin evaluating brand image. If your brand identity paints you as the creator of a breakthrough system for achieving happiness but your readers' reviews dismiss your book as done-before drivel, you have a brand image problem.

Set up Google Alerts for your name and your book title to keep on top of feedback and mentions. Don't be overly concerned about an occasional negative review—you're looking for trends in the feedback more so than one-off observations. A severe gap between brand identity and brand image can be turned around, but it will take time and commitment (and probably the help of a marketing or PR, public relations, firm).

Brand strategy

Once you have an inventory of your brand identity and a sense of your brand image, you can build a brand strategy—a plan to develop the perceived value of your brand. Take a long-term vision and break it down into short-term goals. If you are a vegan cookbook author with aspirations for your own television show, you'll need to plot out milestones for press mentions, increased social media influence, speaking appearances, product development, and so on. The actions prescribed in the brand strategy are essentially the components of your author platform development. Your book-marketing plan also falls under this umbrella since your book is an extension of your brand.

Marketing and branding staff competency

While large companies have many, many people dedicated to marketing and branding, they still identify certain tasks as better handled out of house. It's uncommon for an author or publisher to have a full suite of branding skills within their organization and even more unusual for an author to take a truly objective look at his or her existing brand. While there are certainly aspects of marketing and branding that can be tackled with limited resources, it's important to plan for outsourcing key components that may be better served through external contractors. It's much easier to build on positive brand goodwill than it is to correct a branding misstep, so your branding agents must be top-notch. When evaluating partners, it's critical that they demonstrate a deep understanding of your reader and a sincere interest in the project.

When it comes to platform and brand development, the importance of research and planning can't be stressed enough. Tackling these brand audit components early in the book development process will help ensure that your platform is safely built on a solid foundation.

If you're not sure of the tone and direction of your content, use a blog as research and development to test your concept and see how people react. Through a blog, you can identify your primary, secondary, and even tertiary audiences; establish messaging for each audience; and identify what problems you can solve for them. Encourage your team to research, and provide them with the tools to do so, such as websites for interpreting Amazon sales ranks—or do the research yourself if you have the bandwidth to do so. This type of intel can be pivotal in terms of the overall message of your book.

KEEP YOUR PERSONAL BRAND PERSONAL

Much has been written on the important role a personal brand plays in shaping a thought leader's impact, both on their business and on their wider audience as a whole. A strong personal brand connects a face to the company, which is critical when it comes to helping people relate to (and remember) the brand itself.

A powerful personal brand can be a million-dollar business driver, and an exceptional personal brand can even segue away from a business and into a million-dollar thought leader path lined with books, speaking engagements, and the like (think Gary Vaynerchuk). There are some risks to consider when deciding if you should focus on building your personal brand over a business brand, particularly when it comes to selling a business.

If the personal brand path is right for you, there are five critical elements that set you up for success: authenticity, differentiation, consistency, community, and commitment.

Authenticity

The importance of staying true to your own style and beliefs can't be stressed enough. I have met aspiring authors who have flatly stated something like, "I want to write a book to convey the importance of focusing on business culture as a profit driver." Great! I encourage them to send me an outline and some sample chapters whenever they're ready for a quick review. "Oh," they'll respond, "I'll probably need a ghostwriter. I'm not really sure what to say."

Hold it right there. This is a red flag that this person may not be writing authentically. That will certainly come through in the final book, because it will lack passion. Even with a ghostwriter involved to pound out the words, the fundamental ideas need to come from the author. I would encourage this person to start blogging to gauge whether there's enough content and thought leadership to support a book before making a decision to write a book that isn't coming from the heart.

That's an example from my world, but you get the idea. If it's not true to who you are, it won't be very effective.

Differentiation

Information clutter is rampant. Think about your own behavior when you're taking in a website, a blog, or even search results. You're in speed mode, as you need to be in order to slog through all of the noise. Ultimately, you want your brand to be powerful enough that people share it with others—but first, you've got to get them to stop and take notice.

This ties into authenticity, because chances are good that the differentiation you're struggling to define is right under your nose. Whether it's your experience, your business niche, your customer base, or your style and delivery, it can be hard to see what makes you different on your own. With the help of a branding expert, you can make sure you are clear on this right out of the gate.

Consistency

Once the hard work of defining what sets you apart is done, refer back to it often and stay the course across all platforms. The messaging and visuals (headshots, colors, typeface, etc.) shouldn't vary between your website and social media networks, for example. More importantly, your voice should carry across all of your content. Take every opportunity your audience gives you to share value as an opportunity to simultaneously reinforce your brand.

Community

It's nice to be known, but a truly successful brand takes that a step further and has an army of passionate advocates behind it. While the word *community* has come to represent social media, it really extends well beyond that to capture your customers, your peers, and other like-minded people with an interest in your message.

A thriving community has quantity to provide reach, but it also has quality to drive engagement. Going back to social media as an example, a social media footprint in the millions is not worth much if nobody reacts when you contribute. There will be people who don't like you or what you have to say. Chin up. Focus on serving the advocates and move on.

Commitment

Building a powerful brand with all of the elements mentioned previously takes dedication. Well-known brands are developed over years, even decades. There may be a few shortcuts, but for the most part, it requires a serious commitment of thought, time, and resources (as do most million-dollar ideas).

Taking the initial leap is the fun part. Continuing to chip away at building a brand (especially in times when it feels like nothing is paying off) is where the truly powerful brands pull away from their less-committed competitors. Go into it knowing it's hard work, and plan accordingly.

As the proverb goes, the best time to plant a tree was twenty years ago; the second best time is now.

Put yourself out there

Establishing your platform and who you are as a brand will help pave the way for success. Build your audience around your biggest assets—you and your ideas. Be consistent and authentic in your interactions with your platform. Finally, plan ahead. Get your brand and content strategies in place, and start building now.

Chapter 8

CREATING A PERSONAL CONNECTION

*When given the choice, people will always spend their time
around people they like.*
—Gary Vaynerchuk, *The Thank You Economy*

AFTER YOU'VE ESTABLISHED your platform and who your audience is,
it's important to stay connected. Some of the best ways to do this are
through a strong social media presence, a newsletter, videos, and speaking
engagements. And any of these that you take advantage of should align
with your brand, of course.

ESTABLISH A STRONG SOCIAL MEDIA PRESENCE

In today's thought-leadership world, a social media presence is key. But
to be successful, do you need to have a strong following on every platform? Not necessarily. When starting to write this section, I hesitated to
name any specific platforms at all because I knew that it would anchor
this book in a specific time period. After all, we're not talking about Mys-
pace or Vine these days, and it's very likely that the current social media
platforms will follow the same course.

So, while I will share some basic information about the most important platforms of today, my main focus will be on sharing some social

media best practices that will (I hope) carry over to the platforms of the future.

Getting started

For those with no online presence whatsoever, the idea of jumping in with a full-fledged social media strategy can sound extremely daunting. In addition to writing a book, working full-time, and having a personal life, you also now need to add LinkedIn, Facebook, Twitter, Instagram, and Snapchat to the mix.

Before you stress out, know that you do not need to be a social media dynamo on every platform. If you're just starting out, the best thing that you can do is wade in by doing some basic research. Each platform has a slightly different tone, format, and audience, and it's important to understand what they are.

Spend some time researching the overall demographics of the main players. How old is the average user? Are they primarily men or women? Instagram, for example, skews young among the social media platforms, with double the number of users between the ages of eighteen and twenty-nine compared to LinkedIn.[1]

Now, think about the audience that you're trying to reach with your book. Where are you most likely to find them in the social media landscape?

Another factor to consider beyond basic demographics is the format of each platform. What kind of content are you likely to share? Will you be posting links to recent articles? Maybe you'll be sharing sound bites from your podcast or images from your travels.

To a large degree, the kind of content you share will dictate where you share it. Content with strong visual appeal is going to make the biggest impact somewhere like Instagram or Pinterest, while long-form articles may be best served on LinkedIn. Spend some time paying attention to the kinds of content and conversations being shared on different social media sites. You don't need to reinvent the wheel by creating new content

---

1   Alex York, "Social Media Demographics to Inform a Better Segmentation Strategy," *Sprout Social* (blog), March 6, 2016, https://sproutsocial.com/insights/new-social-media-demographics/#instagram.

specifically for certain platforms, but you should try to share your existing content in a way that will make the most impact.

Plan out your content

Another source of stress for many social media newbies is figuring out what to post and how often to do so. Social media is a rapidly changing landscape, and the idea of constantly churning out new content can deplete your energy fast.

If you've written a book, you're sitting on a goldmine of information that is waiting to be parsed out and shared on social media. Once you have a better understanding of the format required for each forum, you can tailor your existing content to those platforms.

Start off by creating a basic schedule of how often you plan to post. This should be based on two factors: how much content you have to share and how quickly the platform moves. These days, the lifespan of the average tweet is about eighteen minutes.[2] So if you've decided that your audience is on Twitter, posting once a week won't cut it.

Let's say that you've decided to focus on Twitter and LinkedIn and that you've decided to share three tweets per day and one LinkedIn long-form article per week. This is another instance where your editorial calendar will be useful. To save yourself from needing to take a Twitter break every few hours, write out a weekly or monthly schedule of the subject matter you'd like to post and use a scheduling tool like Hootsuite or TweetDeck to send it out automatically. This will not only save you the stress of trying to decide what to share on the fly but will also help you see how often you talk about certain topics.

For instance, if your goal is to drive book sales, a mixture of free content from the book, links to reviews of the book, and calls to action to buy the book will give your audience some variety in the types of posts they see from you. That said, if the lifespan of a tweet is so short and you're sending out a call to action once a month, there's a good chance most of

---

2   Peter Bray, "When Is My Tweet's Prime of Life," *Moz Blog*, November 12, 2012, https://moz.com/blog/when-is-my-tweets-prime-of-life.

your followers will miss it. An editorial calendar can keep you from posting the same things over and over, but it can also help you realize when you've gone too far in the other direction and aren't repeating enough.

All that being said, a little flexibility is important. If a national tragedy happens, a Facebook post celebrating your book may be insensitive. On the flip side, if something new and exciting happens, scrap the social media plan for the day and focus on your exciting news. Because the world of social media moves so quickly, you need to adapt and flow with it.

Connect with people

The entire idea behind social media is to allow people to connect and be "social" in a digital space. With the help of your editorial calendar, you contribute your content to the conversation, but that's only half of the equation. Your audience is looking for engagement from you on social media, and the more people who engage and interact with you on these platforms, the further your reach.

One of the easiest ways to begin forming connections is to share information that is not readily available elsewhere. In other words, let your followers go behind the scenes. Use Instagram Stories, Snapchat, or Facebook Live to speak directly to your audience from wherever you are. Give them a tour of your office, talk about something that you read recently, or let them be a part of a celebration. Do what you think your audience will want to see, but keep the constant calls to action and sales pitches out of it.

Another easy way to build engagement is to respond to comments left on your posts. Take it one step further by sharing and commenting on content similar to yours. Even if you set aside only fifteen minutes a day to do this, it will help to expand your reach by placing you in front of other targeted users.

For authors in particular, a giveaway can be an effective way of establishing a bond with potential readers and turning them into evangelists for your book. Sites like Goodreads make the process of setting up a giveaway even easier by engaging their community of avid readers to participate and giving the winners a platform to post their thoughts about the book right away. Instagram is another great venue for giveaways. Authors can ask entrants to tag a friend in the comments and randomly select a few winners to send books to. Even though there can only be a finite number of winners, the benefit of added visibility from the contest entrants can help drive book sales or preorders.

BUILD A NEWSLETTER

As you're building your audience, it's important to consider how you'll stay in touch with them when they're not on Twitter, Facebook, or your website. Your social media following may be growing, but you're still just one of a million voices showing up in everyone's news feed. There's no guarantee that an audience member will recall why they followed you in the first place if they don't receive content that is engaging, consistent, and sent in a distraction-free space. Arguably *the* best way to check all of these boxes is to start a newsletter.

Though the idea of a newsletter seems archaic to some, it's a ticket into your audience's email inbox, a place they likely visit every day (if not twenty times a day). Whether you share articles you've written, relevant news from your industry, your thoughts on a recent world event, or a mix of all of the above, a newsletter is a chance for you to express yourself to your audience and build their trust.

If the idea of adding one more communication channel to your checklist makes you want to throw in the audience-building towel, take heart. A newsletter can achieve a lot with a little planning and savvy use of content that you already have at your fingertips, and it doesn't have to be long to be effective. When your audience receives well-organized, useful information from you on a consistent basis, they're more likely to engage with you in other venues—and to possibly pay for your product or service.

It will take time for your newsletter to capture your personality and for you to find a comfortable rhythm and style, so don't be discouraged if it doesn't feel like you're hitting the mark on the first try. What matters most is starting. Setting a schedule for yourself, building an email list, and mapping out what content you want to use are useful tools for beginning a successful newsletter.

Mark your calendar

By taking the time to plan your content in advance, you'll save yourself hours that might otherwise be spent staring at a blank screen or scrambling to collect content at the last minute.

Decide on a frequency that will fit your schedule (perhaps weekly, monthly, or quarterly) and that makes sense for the rhythm of your work. An author writing a 900-page novel may be better off with a quarterly progress update, while a social media marketer will want to share thoughts on industry news every week or so. Once you've decided on a timeline, stick to it. If you're meeting someone in person and want to earn their trust, you show up when you say you will. The same logic applies to newsletters.

As you're creating your calendar, identify seasonal or industry tie-ins you could include in future newsletters. What extra value could you offer your audience during the holidays, while the Olympics are going on, or when your industry is gearing up for a huge conference? By looking to the future, you give yourself time to create new content, and the space to fill on your calendar looks less daunting.

Build your list

Your newsletter needs somewhere to go, so you'll need to build an email list. The challenge in this task, of course, is that we're all wary of giving out our email addresses for fear of being spammed with irrelevant information or endless pleas to buy something.

You can help incentivize your audience to share email addresses by offering a useful digital gift through your website. It could be a trial of new software you've developed, free access to an online class you offer, or the first chapter of your book in exchange for an email address. Make it clear that the address is for your newsletter, and announce your offer on social media to drive traffic to your website.

Conferences, speaking engagements, and webinars are also great opportunities to invite people to sign up for your newsletter. When you have a captive audience who is engaged with what you're talking about, it's a great time to offer a way to continue engaging with you.

Once someone has given you their email address, treat it with care. This is not your opportunity to send every sales offer you have; that's a recipe for an unfollow. If you treat your audience's time with respect and keep emails to a (consistent) minimum, they're more likely to pay attention when you are ready to share an offer.

Compile your content

A newsletter is a blank slate for you to express your personality and focus on the topics that are most important to you and your audience. In a short update you can—

- Address readers' pain points: Share how-tos, tactics, infographics, and tutorials.
- Be a content curator and thought leader: Share relevant industry news and your perspective and insights.
- Encourage engagement: Share details about upcoming conferences, speaking events, and book signings.
- Create strong digital content: Share a video series or host webinars to engage readers across formats.

If any of that seems intimidating, shift your thinking to make compiling content enjoyable. When you find an interesting article or a well-designed infographic, save it to add to a future newsletter. Subscribe to the newsletters of a few of your peers and competitors, and get to know the conversations that are taking place in your field. Figure out where your voice fits in the conversation, and find content you've already written that supports your points.

Some people use a newsletter as an opportunity to share their thoughts on a current topic in traditional letter form (and that may be the right style for you), but in general, it's best to make a list of relevant content that is short and to the point. Summarize each piece you share with key takeaways and calls to action to ensure that readers who spend only a moment scanning the letter will still get value out of it.

If you do decide to write a long-form letter, short and sweet should still be your mantra. Try not to exceed five paragraphs, and make sure that every word counts toward the point you're making. Include links to articles or helpful websites throughout your text to catch the attention of those who skim, and make sure that your opening and closing lines demonstrate the value of your message.

A newsletter is an opportunity to grow your relationship with your audience in an undistracted setting. When you keep the value of your content for your specific audience in the forefront of your mind as you create each newsletter, you'll begin to look forward to the opportunity to share. If you're excited about your topic, your curated audience will be too.

CREATE VIDEOS TO CONNECT

Outside of one-to-one connection, video is the most powerful way to add interest to your website, demonstrate your expertise and speaking skills, and connect with your audience on a personal level. Currently, videos are also the leading way to boost your online impact. According to Eyeview, including a video on your home page can increase conversions by 80 percent or more.[3] And when it comes to efficiently communicating a message, Forrester researcher Dr. James McQuivey estimates that one minute of video is equal to 1.8 million words.[4]

Don't let that discourage you from writing your book—remember that video is a way to expand your message to reach a different audience, and the book will give you the core content to translate into video format. Strong video content adds value in several other ways as well:

---

3   Insivia, "27 Video Stats for 2017," January 27, 2017, http://www.insivia. com/27-video-stats-2017/.

4   Modulates.com, "A Minute of Video Is Worth 1.8 Million Words, According to Forrester Research," April 17, 2014, http://www.marketwired.com/press-release/a-minute-of-video-is-worth-18-million-words-according-to-forrester-research-1900666.html.

- It highlights your expertise. Seeing and hearing you in action solidifies you as an expert.

- It demonstrates your speaking skills. It's imperative for aspiring authors to have a few video samples of live speaking.

- It shows off your personality. Sometimes it's hard to capture a certain sense of humor or air of authority in the written word. Video helps you and your unique personality shine through.

- It provides worth. Most importantly, it gives your audience something of value, whether it's information or entertainment.

Creating videos isn't difficult—just follow a few basic steps to start sharing your expertise with the world.

Equipment

First, you need a computer and either a video camera or a high-quality phone or computer camera. You can also rent professional equipment from media rental outlets for as little as thirty dollars a day—a good idea if you're planning to knock out a bunch of videos at once.

Your computer and camera likely have embedded microphones. However, if you plan to work in areas with a great deal of background noise or if you want to record at public events, an external microphone is a solid investment. A decent external microphone costs less than fifty dollars and will make the difference between a tolerable video with distracting, unclear noise and a professional-sounding video that lets the viewer focus on your content, not any production shortcomings.

Once you shoot your video, you'll need to edit for corrections, flow, and length and to add music and stills as appropriate. Typically, you'll need to build an introduction (intro) and closing (outro). The intro will include consistent music, your picture or the cover of your book, and the name of the video or video series. The outro will have all of the above plus a call to action, most likely a link to buy the book online.

Head over to ideasinfluenceandincome.com for a list of video editing tools, along with royalty-free music, stock photography resources, and sample intros and outros to use as learning tools.

Location and setting

Where you film is every bit as important as what you use to film. You don't need to build out a major studio in order to develop high-quality, compelling videos. You just need to follow a few key guidelines.

When filming, choose a location with bright natural light and minimal background noise. Indoors and outdoors are both fine so long as you are well lit, are void of glare, and can control the amount of chatter and interruptions occurring around you.

Bear in mind that the microphone can pick up a lot of background noise, like trains, doors slamming, and loud voices. Your brain does a good job of filtering those out, but the microphone may deal you a few surprises if you're not in a controlled environment. To avoid those surprises, consider hiring a professional videographer for the day, as that person should be able to identify problematic noise interference.

Use professional lighting and a backdrop that is neutral in color—well-lit white and cream work best for indoors. If you are outdoors, choose either a wall that is light colored or an open, naturally well-lit location.

Minimize or eliminate clutter to keep the focus on you. If you are filming in an office, remove excess paper, food, notes, and other unnecessary items that can detract from you and your message.

Place yourself front and center if you are speaking solo. Position the camera so the focus is on your face and upper torso, just as it would be if you were standing face-to-face with someone. Only use full-body angles if you are demonstrating a physical activity.

Content

Online videos are generally short bursts of information that run roughly two to five minutes, but under some circumstances they can be longer. Think of your videos as teasers for your book, speaking topics, or workshops. They should provide key nuggets of standalone, useful information. Good content includes—

- How to: A short demonstration or step-by-step instruction (e.g., "How to Make Videos in Three Simple Steps" or "How to Improve Your Speaking Skills")

- Best of: A short video highlighting the top three to seven traits, skills, or practices of a function or industry (e.g., "The Top Three Traits of a Great Leader" or "Seven Ways to Motivate a Team")

- Interview: A short interview or excerpt of an interview demonstrating your ability to communicate with the media unscripted

Integrating video into your marketing efforts

A robust platform-building strategy uses video in multiple ways, maximizing your visibility online and fleshing out your presence with differentiated content. You can take advantage of this powerful medium through video blogging, your social media platform(s), your website, or the use of book trailers.

VIDEO BLOGGING

Video blogging lets you harness the power of video and blogging in one media format. Just like traditional text blog posts, you can post videos on your blog to share ideas, insights, and observations. You can mix video posts in with text posts or build out your entire blog based solely on video. Video blogs are expected to be casual, conversational, and short. Host these on a YouTube channel dedicated to you and your content, and embed the YouTube-hosted video on your site to make it easy for you and your viewers.

You don't need to go crazy with the production quality, but again, be sure to use a microphone and shoot in a well-lit space! YouTube offers many tools to help edit, add music and captioning, and so on.

SOCIAL MEDIA

To maximize views for your videos, share links on your Facebook, Twitter, and LinkedIn feeds.

Google owns YouTube, and YouTube videos have a tremendous impact on search results. The following strategies can help you maximize your video presence on YouTube.

As mentioned earlier, create a channel dedicated to your brand. This will be the home for all of your videos.

Create SEO- and user-friendly titles for your videos. Search engine optimization, or SEO, is the process of increasing the traffic to your website or online content through strategic efforts to impact search engine results. Titles like "How to Make Videos in Three Easy Steps" or "Five Tips to Boost Your SEO Today" are more likely to grab a viewer's attention than a simple description. Use Google's AdWords research tools to find potential words for your title with the strongest SEO results still relevant to your content.

Add descriptions and "long-tail" keywords to each video. A long-tail keyword is highly specific or niche in nature, such as *nonprofit leadership skills* instead of just *leadership*.

Create captions or scripts for your videos to boost their SEO results. YouTube offers a captioning service, or check out the captioning resources listed at ideasinfluenceandincome.com. These services add a time-coded text transcript of your video, which gives Google and YouTube comprehensive information about the content of your video. For example, if someone searches for a phrase mentioned in the video and you have posted a transcript of the video, Google may include your video in search results and may even start the video at the point where the search phrase is used.

Add your website address at the end of each video during the editing process so people who find you through Google or YouTube have easy access to your website.

WEBSITE

Videos add interest to your site and are a great way to add more valuable content and search relevance. Post a welcome video on your home page, share your interviews on your author bio page, and show off your demonstrations and how-tos on your speaker page.

BOOK TRAILERS

Book trailers have become an increasingly popular way to advertise a new release. Just like a movie trailer, a book trailer provides a teaser for an upcoming book. They can be spread through social media, posted on your website, and used for ad placement on certain online outlets. The most effective book trailers are short, to the point, funny, or emotionally powerful. The "show, don't tell" rule you learned in your writing classes, which enables the reader to experience the story through action rather than description, is even more relevant in a video format.

Some authors prefer to do multiple short videos highlighting key concepts from their book in lieu of a book trailer. Focus on teaching just one to three key points, and keep it under three minutes if possible. These "teaching videos" are a great way to highlight the breadth of your knowledge while creating a person-to-person connection.

There are countless ways to create and share content. You can maximize all of them by focusing on delivering value to your audience, taking the time to edit and review your videos, and committing to accepting feedback as you continue to grow and refine your author platform.

SPEAK

Speaking can take many forms, ranging all the way from wedding toasts to informal presentations with your team at work to TEDx talks and lucrative keynote corporate speaking gigs.

Whatever the format, what all of these speaking engagements have in common is the unique opportunity for you to build a strong connection with an audience based on the combination of your content and your inimitable personal brand. Speaking provides a person-to-person bond that is hard to replicate.

For many business leaders, the corporate keynote presentation is the holy grail of making an impact and adding to their "tribe," or community of supporters. There are plenty of resources to help you develop an amazing keynote presentation and then land some prime opportunities to present it to the right audience. (Visit ideasinfluenceandincome.com to learn more.)

One word of warning: Your book will not automatically translate into a speech (and vice versa). Don't simply grab a chapter of your book and memorize it as a keynote address. As I've said, the spoken word is a different art form. The delivery, phrasing, and flow of a speech make for a unique form of expression. Listen to a speech that has moved you, and then just read the text. The words may still be powerful, but they will be flat compared to the recorded speech.

Professional speechwriters are masters of this craft, and it's worth hiring one to make sure your keynote is polished and powerful. The Professional Speechwriters Association is a good place to start if you're looking for help on this front.

Speaker-specific professional organizations like Toastmasters and the National Speakers Association (or NSA) offer local chapters and regular meetings to help refine your presentation and build your speaking career.

NSA (they jokingly call themselves the NSA that speaks, not the one that listens!) organizes an annual conference that is worth attending to meet other speakers, learn about the craft and business of speaking, and stay on top of other developments in the industry. NSA is also a good place to connect with a speaking coach and representatives from major speakers' bureaus to determine if their services are right for you.

As a heads-up on speakers' bureaus, you will hear as much negative feedback on working with them as you will hear positive. It's a feedback loop similar to that of author and traditional publisher in some ways. Established speakers feel that bureaus take an unreasonable cut for serving as a middleman when it's the speaker doing the hustling to earn the gig—just as some authors feel they do all the work to build their audience and sell books while the publisher takes a big cut.

In both cases, there is a lot of time invested behind the scenes that you may not appreciate if you haven't been in the business. Going it alone teaches that to many people, who then realize their time is not best spent handling the minutia that a speakers' bureau (or traditional publisher) handles on your behalf.

And a meeting planner for a major conference will probably reach out to a bureau to find their next opening-night speaker, but they probably will not reach out directly to you (unless you're quite famous). It's your job to help the bureau understand what makes you different and marketable and which audience you intend to serve. The clearer that is, the more likely you are to have a successful and lucrative bureau relationship.

If it doesn't conflict with any speakers' bureaus you work with, consider conducting an influencer mailing to your intended speaking outlets with a clear call to action and ancillary materials like your book, a flash drive with video of you speaking, and memorable tchotchkes. Don't be discouraged if you don't get many responses at first. Be confident that you're putting in the legwork to spread the word about how you bring value, and be persistent!

Once you have that golden opportunity at hand, don't blow the chance to leverage it for all its worth in terms of building your platform. Deliver a keynote worthy of a standing ovation, but then capture that enthusiasm and engagement to strengthen your brand and create future opportunities. To start on your path to being a smarter and better speaker, you need to be prepared, execute, and then follow up.

Preparation

The best speakers have a core message that they customize to their keynote audience. Smart speakers will work with a meeting planner to best understand who will be sitting in the audience, what pressing problem they collectively face, and how the speaker's experience relates to those things.

For example, a sales performance speaker can gather some intel from the meeting planner about the team's prior year performance and work that into his or her presentation. Recent awards, milestones, or other public recognition are usually easy enough to research online and weave into your talk. These little touches make you less generic, and they help to forge a stronger connection since you have personalized your message to your audience.

Execution

During the talk itself, smart speakers will leverage both their book and a feedback form.

The best way to get your book into your audience's hands is to work it into the terms of your speaking fee up front. The meeting planner will arrange to buy a book for each audience member. If that sale runs through retail channels, the speaker will also receive a royalty for each book sold.

For self-published and hybrid authors, if you own your books by virtue of paying for their production, you probably will have a choice to make here. You can sell the books directly to the meeting planner or conference and pocket all of the proceeds, or you can run the sales through retail (via a book retailer or a bulk sale service like 800-CEO-READ) to boost your auditable sales history as tracked by Nielsen BookScan, the industry's tool for measuring retail sell-through.

BookScan is a tool I touched on in the *Ideas* section of this book, and you will see it come up several times in this book. There are many uses for BookScan that authors, publishers, and booksellers will find helpful, so if you're not familiar with this tool, I encourage you to explore the wealth of information it can provide.

Your BookScan history will be important if you want to do multiple books (both in terms of negotiating a strong deal and gaining solid retail distribution), but if you are a one-and-done author, it may not matter as much to you.

Moving on to the day of the speech, providing a well-thought-out, branded feedback form (pens!) is another way to convert that audience into part of your larger platform. Include an area where they can provide an endorsement or blurb about your talk (and let them check a box giving permission for you to use it in promotional materials). On the same form, you can ask for their email address if they would like to subscribe to your newsletter.

Finally, be bold and use the feedback form to ask your audience if they are aware of any other events or companies where your keynote would resonate. Reaching out to those new leads is much easier when you can say someone who heard you speak suggested the potential match.

Create your form so that the audience can tear off the feedback portion and return it to you while holding on to the other portion, which should include your website and social media contact info for their reference.

Follow up

After giving a speech, it's important that you don't let those important connections you might have made dissipate. Most events and conferences have a designated hashtag to help organize social media mentions. Using that hashtag is a great way to make sure the attendees see your profile and know how to connect with you online, and the meeting planners will definitely appreciate your efforts to engage. At a minimum, post a thank you message on social media right after your talk, using the event hashtag.

After your presentation, move all of the information from your feedback forms into whatever system you use to manage your content or lead generation. It's a nice touch to send a quick email note of appreciation to those who agreed to sign up for your newsletter.

And of course, send a follow-up note of thanks to the meeting planner or person who booked you to appear in the first place. Open the door for feedback and suggestions from them as well—sometimes attendees will be reluctant to share negative (or constructive) feedback about your talk directly with you, so the meeting planner may be the only way to hear that commentary.

Gaining traction as a professional speaker takes time and hustle. You need to do much more than show up and speak to do it well and build future opportunities.

As you build your author platform as a speaker, watch for cues from your audience feedback to help you determine the content behind your next keynote. Good speakers regularly produce new content. The same old speech only goes so far!

Keep your new content true to your brand, but hit a different note. Speakers like Simon Sinek and Tim Ferriss do this well. Ferriss, for instance, gained fame with *The Four-Hour Work Week*. From there, he expanded his brand to *The Four-Hour Chef* and *The Four-Hour Body*.

They are all essentially books about productivity and life hacks, just with a slightly different spin intended to serve a new audience.

Listening to your audience to discover these additional opportunities will help ensure that your speaking career grows with time, bringing your author platform up alongside it.

Now get moving

Before you start hustling speaking gigs, get your promotional materials in order. You just need a couple of things to start—a speaker press kit and a video of you speaking.

A speaker press kit functions as a one-sheet that easily communicates your value as a speaker and the subject matter in which you have expertise. It will include a summary of what you speak on, your background, a headshot, a handful of testimonials about your speaking prowess, and your contact info.

This document should be easily downloadable via your website and should look just as good printed as it does digitally.

As you land speaking engagements, be sure to capture them on video (with your client's permission). This footage can be spliced into a sizzle reel to help an event planner get a feel for your energy and envision you speaking at their next event.

These materials, along with your contact information, should be housed in a section of your website clearly marked "Speaking."

Creating a strong personal connection with your audience and staying engaged is vital to the success of your book and your brand. Start with what you're good at and get creative. If you're inspired by your content and you let that passion shine through in the ways you reach out using different platforms, your audience will be inspired too.

Chapter 9

LEVERAGING YOUR PLATFORM

Alone we can do so little; together we can do so much.
—Helen Keller

IT'S EASY TO FEEL OVERWHELMED by the daunting task of building a platform. It requires plenty of strategy, time, and effort to connect with an audience and then keep them close so that they're ready to convert into buyers when it's time for your product launch.

To lighten this burden, think about connecting with groups of people rather than individuals . . . and if you do focus on individuals, focus your time on nurturing relationships with people who can extend the results of your efforts by bringing you into an even bigger group or community. I call this *focusing on faucets*.

Once you turn a faucet on, you can walk away, and it will keep delivering water. You don't have to retrieve and dump bucket after bucket of water into your tub to fill it. The most efficient way to build your platform is by identifying potential faucet relationships and turning them on, leaving you to focus on the other demands for your time.

As an example, at Greenleaf Book Group, we work closely with our authors' outside literary agents and publicists. These industry colleagues are often the first point of contact for a writer who is exploring the idea of publishing a book. We have spent years cultivating relationships and friendships with our publicist and agent friends so that when they encounter an author who might be a good fit for our model, they think of us and make an introduction. For our company, publicists and agents are faucets who bring us many great prospective authors on a repeat basis.

Of course, even a faucet relationship requires an investment of time to build and nurture. Whether it's grabbing a cup of coffee in person when you pass through town or sending them a Starbucks gift card to grab a cup on you in absentia, showing a commitment to the partnership and an interest in the person and their work will help to strengthen your bond.

Now that you understand the idea behind focusing on faucets, let's try to identify those opportunities. As you read through this section, I encourage you to take notes and start thinking through these four areas of potential faucets to support your audience-building efforts.

Vendors

The businesses that are your customers can also be strong lead faucets. Depending on the type of work they do, they may have a good understanding of your expertise and the audience you intend to reach. A warm referral from someone who knows you and your work can be very powerful.

For example, if you are a social media guru who has hired a web design company to build a new site for you, that same web design company may be an excellent faucet for you. The web design firm probably has other customers who are asking about online visibility, keyword optimization, social media integration, and other related areas that are in your wheelhouse but perhaps not theirs.

Complementary businesses

Complementary businesses are those that operate in a space that fits alongside what you do without competing with it. The example I gave earlier of literary agents and publicists supporting Greenleaf Book Group falls in this category.

When building out a list of opportunities in this category, stay focused on complementary businesses that serve the same core client as you do. Your faucet is only effective if it brings in the right type of leads.

Complementary competitors

Ah, the competition. The notion of leaning on your competitors for referrals might make the hair on your neck stand up a bit, but hear me out on this one.

You have direct competitors, and you have complementary competitors. Your direct competitors are going after the same core client as you are. Your complementary competitors provide similar services to you but pursue a different core client. They may be approached by a client who isn't right for them but would be perfect for you—and you want to be the first person the competitor thinks of when they realize they need to make a referral.

Many of the public speakers I work with support each other in this way. A leadership speaker with a brand built around her military background may be asked to come into a company to do a keynote on working with the millennial generation. She knows this is not her area of expertise, so she will refer a complementary competitor—another speaker who specializes in exactly this type of content. The customer will be thrilled to have the vetting done for them, and the speaker she referred will most certainly return the favor when the opportunity arises.

Professional organizations and associations

An association is usually seen as the authority and ultimate resource for its industry. Associations work to build industries, support their members, and think about trends and initiatives that might impact the industry's future. The strong ones enjoy strength in numbers and longevity that make them very visible as a brand connected to your area of expertise.

To be a member of your industry's association extends its credibility to you. That alone can make it worth joining.

As importantly, your future customers may be starting their search for a business partner with your industry's primary association. So beyond joining the association, consider getting involved at a deeper level so that you become part of that community versus just another member. Speak at a conference, volunteer at an event, or write an article for their member newsletter. With professional organizations, you tend to get out what you put in, and a small investment of time can be enough to keep your name and unique value proposition front-of-mind when the association is called upon for a referral.

These faucet partners belong in a different category in your strategic platform-building plan than initiatives like publicity and advertising. Faucet partners require personal connections and relationships to work. Publicity and advertising fall into more of a "spray-and-pray" bucket, where you have a one-off advertisement or media hit and capitalize on the short-term attention that brings to you. Both are legitimate strategies, and how you balance them within your own outreach plan will depend on your goals, time, and resources.

NO LEAKY FAUCETS!

We've established that faucet partnerships require more relationship building (read: more time investment) but can have multiple long-term payouts. If you've made the choice to focus on this area, you need to have systems in place to manage both the relationships and the leads. The tools that help you in this area are like the plumbing behind the faucet. Neglect them and you may spring a leak that wastes precious resources.

To avoid a faucet leak, you must ask yourself whether you are the right person to manage this part of your strategy. It may be the case that budget requires you to be that person, in addition to everything else you are managing. Given the personal nature of expert brand building, the person to handle this would ideally be you. As a bonus, you then don't have to worry about relationships one day walking out the door along with a person who quits working for you.

But if you know that building and maintaining relationships are not your strengths or that you absolutely do not have time to do this, and you have the resources to enlist help, look for someone who can ride shotgun with you on these faucet initiatives. That assistance can be especially valuable in the research stage.

Just remember that we're trying to build your name, your brand, and your reputation. If someone helps with outreach, be sure that your name is always tied into the outreach. Participate in important calls when you can, even if you don't take the lead. And make sure that gifts and email campaigns are set up to be from you, not the person who is helping.

Managing faucets

To keep your faucets in good working order, you need to practice regular maintenance.

Strong relationships require regular touch points. This is less of a priority if you have a referral agreement in place and there's compensation for the lead your partner sends you. As you develop your strategy in this area, consider whether you intend to manage these relationships as handshake agreements, relying on goodwill and your partner's intent to serve the potential referee well, or if you'd prefer to add an extra incentive for the referral in the form of a referral (or finder's) fee.

A finder's fee can certainly help keep you top of mind for your partners, but it may not be the right choice in all scenarios. The exchange of money for a referral creates a financial relationship that should be disclosed, by ethical standards. It can also create some tension down the road should things not go well.

Consider a scenario where a fellow author or speaker recommends you for a gig and you pay that referring speaker a portion of the resulting keynote fee, an arrangement that you make the customer aware of. Naturally, this next part won't happen in real life, but let's pretend you absolutely bomb the keynote. Now the customer is upset with both you and the referring speaker, since both of you were paid for this disastrous result, and multiple relationships are left damaged in the wake of this situation.

As you go into your partnership outreach, know that some of your potential partners will resist financial incentives for this reason—especially if they don't know you or your work very well. If that's the case, you'll need to rely on relationship management to keep that referral source active.

Relationship management can take many forms. You can sponsor their events, support them on social media by sharing and liking their content, make in-person visits when you are in town, copresent at trade shows, provide content for their blog or newsletter, or use a CRM (customer relationship management) tool like Salesforce or Contactually to just periodically check in and say hello.

Partners will require a different approach based on their unique business and content needs. As you explore these partnerships and where you can create value, use your CRM tool to make notes about their needs (especially areas where you can contribute content to help serve their audience) and your own next steps around frequency of follow-up. You may put some partners on a monthly touch point schedule and others on a quarterly routine. Automate as much of it as you can without losing the personal touch that keeps the relationship authentic.

Chapter 10

READY FOR LAUNCH

There is only one thing in the world worse than being talked about,
and that is not being talked about.
—Oscar Wilde

NOW THAT YOU'VE ESTABLISHED YOUR BRAND AND PLATFORM, and you've written your book, it's finally time to publish. Before your book launches, you need to have a strong website and a marketing plan in place. When your pub date arrives, you will need a strategic plan in place to get the most out of it. You also need to think about how you're going to keep your audience engaged after your book has published. How are you going to keep that momentum and continue to expand your audience? If you're properly prepared, this goal is a lot more attainable.

CURATE A WELL-DESIGNED WEBSITE

Considering all of the hard work put into creating your book, it's critically important to have a well-designed and current website to reinforce the quality of your content and brand. Your website is the hub of your platform and a vehicle for conveying your brand to both media and readers. It is also a tool for building your community of followers and creating a link between you and your book. A memorable, effective website is crucial to your platform and must be designed to bring mutual benefit to you and your audience.

The first thing you need is a relevant and easy-to-spell URL. The web address you select should ideally be your name (or some iteration of your name, like JohnDoeAuthor.com) or possibly the title of your book (or some iteration of that, like BookTitleBook.com). The latter is an especially good option if you know you're only writing one book, but even if you write another book, it's easy enough to buy a URL specific to that new title and redirect it to your existing author website.

URLs are inexpensive, so in the interest of ensuring that people who search for you can find you, it's a worthwhile investment to buy multiple URLs using variations of your name, your book title, and your company name, if applicable, and redirecting all of those URLs to your main site.

Most people will use a keyword search to find your website, so keep it succinct and avoid any unusual words, nontraditional spellings, or phrases that might make it difficult to search correctly or even remember.

After you've secured your URL(s), there are certain elements you should consider adding for an effective author website.

Welcome or home page

Your welcome or home page is the first thing your audience will see when they visit your website. On this page, you feature your name, your brand promise, and a high-quality headshot. The home page is also where you should highlight the strongest of any third-party endorsements, if you have them.

Adding website visitors to your email list is a priority, so incorporate a prominent newsletter sign-up option on the home page. Many authors offer premium content downloads (exclusive resources or original work only available to subscribers) as an incentive to drive newsletter enrollment.

On the rest of the site, move the newsletter sign-up option to the footer of every page along with your social media hyperlink icons and "buy" links to help visitors easily engage with you and purchase your products online.

About the author

Your author bio should be all about you—go into more detail about yourself, your experience, and the credentials that establish you as the authority in your field. Start with the biographical detail that backs up your professional expertise, then close with some details about your hobbies or family that help your audience connect with you, the person, versus you, the professional.

Sample work

Just as it sounds, a sample work page is where you should provide sample excerpts or links to your work. Make sure that all documents are formatted professionally and reflect your brand. A well-designed PDF is the easiest option to make a sample or excerpt available as a direct download.

Many book retailers also offer website plug-ins or code to embed their excerpts directly onto your site. You can also simply hyperlink to the third-party listings for your book that feature sample content.

Services

Some authors choose to incorporate their service offerings into the contact or author bio sections of their website, while others use a separate page to highlight those professional services. There is no right or wrong answer here; it ultimately depends on how appropriate the act of directly offering services feels to your audience—and to you.

If it is appropriate to have a standalone services page on your site, use it to highlight how your speaking, online courses, coaching, and so on can extend beyond the content offered in your book. Give specific examples of keynote titles and takeaways, areas of coaching expertise, and any other persuasive content that will help to convert your website visitor into a client.

Whenever possible, include praise from clients who have hired you for your services, and be sure to include a link to a contact form directly from this page so that you can easily capture interested visitors.

News and events

Use your author pressroom (also sometimes labeled a *media* page) to highlight the attention you've earned from television, print, radio, and online mentions. This is critical to convince certain people of your relevance—especially other media, who don't have the time to otherwise vet you!

Post all media mentions, such as upcoming appearances, workshops, book signings, and podcasts, and develop a press kit that media can download and use.

Blog

The primary goal in all of your efforts to create influence is to build an engaged audience base. Make it easy by creating an interactive element to your site that lets them establish dialogue with you and other followers from your community.

Maintaining an engaging blog is definitely a commitment. To nurture an audience, you need to continually put new content in front of them to keep the conversation alive. Expect to post on a regular schedule, ideally a few times a month at a minimum. Again, work this into your editorial calendar so you're not left scrambling to come up with content at the last minute. If that feels unmanageable, leave the blog page off your site. It's better to have no blog at all than to have one that is neglected.

If you think you will have somewhat consistent new content but not enough to warrant a blog, consider giving those ideas a home on your website with a different name, like *Learning Center*, that does not convey an expectation of regular updates. Using that phrase removes the anticipation of consistency that comes with the word *blog* but still provides a place to share meaningful updates and new content with all of the corresponding SEO benefit.

Contact page

Your contact page should be all business. Provide your email address or a form for guests to submit inquiries. If it applies to you, be sure to also include your publisher and publicist contact details.

If speaking is a part of your business, include your downloadable speaker press kit on this page and a contact link to your agent or bureau, if applicable.

As your brand evolves, so should your website. Keep it relevant, timely, and current with content and media updates.

As the hub of your platform-building activities, your website should be an ongoing focus in terms of new content and general updates for your audience. It's the first place people will go to learn mcre about you, so capitalize on their visits by making a solid impression that demonstrates your commitment to serving them and their interest in your work.

PUBLICITY

The art of creating a book sometimes leaves the business of launching it on the back burner. Fueled by passion and commitment, the author puts blinders on and plods away at a manuscript with one goal in mind: MUST FINISH BOOK. Quite often, it's only when the pencil is finally put down that the author starts to think about marketing and launching the book. Unfortunately, that's way too late.

As I've hopefully impressed upon you by now, the key to having a smooth, strategic book launch is to plan far in advance and begin platform building as early as possible. Part of this process is to explore and determine whether you will work with a publicist to help generate media coverage like radio, print, and television interviews.

Hire a publicist

Authors often ask me if hiring a publicist is worth the investment. For the majority of books, I would say yes. A successful publicity campaign can bring in a level of media coverage that lands more clients, more brand cachet, more book sales, and additional media opportunities. That makes hiring an outside publicity firm with experience in your industry a big decision, and knowing what to expect on the front end can help you make the right selection and get more out of the experience. If you're considering hiring a publicist, here are a few things you should keep in mind.

A GOOD PUBLICIST WILL FIND MULTIPLE ANGLES TO USE WHEN PITCHING YOUR STORY

Each media outlet serves a different segment of your audience in a different way, so the hook of the publicity pitch needs to be tailored to their demographics and the tone of their content.

Having multiple angles in your pitching arsenal is also necessary in case what seemed to be the most obvious angle just isn't working. Whether due to a general lack of interest or competing current events, sometimes a pivot to a different angle can make or break a campaign.

A PUBLICIST DOES NOT BURN VALUABLE JOURNALIST RELATIONSHIPS WITH OFF-TARGET PITCHES

A publicist's contacts, and his or her relationship with those contacts, mean everything to the success of the pitch. Journalists are inundated with pitches from publicists who use a "spray and pray" approach to getting the word out versus thoughtful, well-crafted pitches that are built with the journalists' audience in mind. For that reason, resist the urge to push your publicist to blast a useless press release. Work with them to find the most intriguing parts of your story and zero in on finding the audience that really cares.

A GOOD PUBLICIST IS STRATEGIC ABOUT THE ORDER IN WHICH THEY PITCH THE MEDIA

In many cases, major outlets want an exclusive. So if you write a great opinion piece or information article, for example, your publicist would typically give the major publications first run at picking it up before approaching smaller outlets. This way, you're getting maximum impact out of that content.

A PUBLICIST FOLLOWS UP WITH CREATIVITY AND DIPLOMACY

It's a rare pitch that captures a journalist's attention at first glance. Journalists are busy trying to stay on top of current events and trends, plus the never-ending pitches from sources known and unknown.

A good publicist will follow up with an added bit of relevance or demographic info to add new life to the pitch, and the publicist should provide you (and whoever else you feel needs it) with a weekly update detailing their pitches and follow-up efforts.

A PUBLICIST DOES NOT DETERMINE WORLD EVENTS

Unfortunately, sometimes the odds are not in your favor. Timing is critical to the success of a publicity campaign. It's important to consider holidays, tie-ins, anniversaries, and other known events and important dates as you strategize your big push.

Even with highly thought-out timing and strategy, a campaign can be completely derailed by the weight of other newsworthy stories that simply monopolize the headlines. Major events like presidential elections will predictably dominate the news for a good length of time, but unforeseen events like natural disasters or celebrity deaths can also deal an unexpected blow to publicity efforts in certain media outlets.

A GOOD PUBLICIST WILL TELL YOU WHAT YOU MAY NOT WANT TO HEAR

When choosing a publicist, stay away from the yes-man. You may need a dose of tough love from your publicist to ensure your expectations are reasonable. (We all think our stories are great, after all, and it's hard to imagine that someone doesn't care, isn't it?)

Your publicist also needs to be frank with you about the areas where you need polish, whether that's speaking on camera or being able to quickly crank out a great opinion article concerning trends in your business when a journalist requests it. Heed their advice, and work out those rough spots so that you make the most of these opportunities when they do arrive.

Like so many powerful relationships, the most effective publicists serve as partners to help you grow your brand. Keeping these points in mind will help ensure a smooth start and better working relationship so you can stay focused on your moment in the spotlight.

Going it alone

Every author wants to land that prime piece of media coverage to boost their visibility, credibility, and sales. As Jane Russell said, "Publicity can be terrible. But only if you don't have any." Of course, hiring a publicist is expensive. If funds prohibit engaging a publicist to support your book launch, it's better to try it on your own than to do nothing at all—as long as you approach it strategically. Here are some tips to increase your likelihood of scoring powerful publicity.

TAILOR YOUR PITCH TO THE REPORTER'S PUBLICATION AND THEIR BEAT

Reporters are slammed with pitches, sometimes upward of a hundred per day. They can smell a "spray and pray" mass pitch in no time flat and will throw it in the "pass" pile just as quickly.

Take the time to customize your pitch to be appropriate for the media outlet you're targeting. This means you'll need to think about their viewer or reader demographics and spin the pitch angle so that it resonates with that group. Make yourself familiar with their programming and stay close to that tone.

Additionally, larger outlets may have multiple reporters whom you'd like to pitch, with each handling a different beat. For instance, a growing health-oriented start-up might consider pitching separate reporters for the business and health beats at the same publication . . . and the pitch should be modified accordingly for these different audiences.

PROVIDE PROOF OF CONCEPT

Busy reporters don't have time to research you, your company, or your performance. Ultimately, they are looking for content that will drive views and readership—so establish that there's demand for your story as soon as possible.

If you can point to a wave of awards, other recent media coverage, or growth numbers, working those into your pitch will help the reporter understand why an audience will care about your story and why it is news.

KEEP IT SUCCINCT

Your pitch will be considered and reviewed in minutes, if not seconds. Set aside some time to write just the first few sentences of your pitch. Then rewrite them and rewrite them again, until these sentences hit the reader over the head with the compelling point of your pitch. If you don't hook the reporter quickly, you don't stand a chance to land coverage.

MAKE THE REPORTER'S JOB EASY

Don't you love it when someone walks into your office with a problem and then presents a well-thought-out solution or two for your consideration? Of course you do. It makes your job easier.

The same is true of reporters. The easier you can make it for them to pull together the story, the better. For example, note who is available for an interview and whether you have license-free footage or images available that could be used to build out the piece.

DON'T CALL

No reporter is going to pick up the phone and take your pitch. Send an email or connect with the reporter via social media (Twitter is great for this), and ask how they prefer to be pitched.

TIE YOUR PITCH TO AN EVENT OR ANNIVERSARY

Media outlets often run stories around themes related to holidays, events, or anniversaries. Use tools like National Day Calendar to find day, week, or month observations that can be tied into your story. (Think "National Small Business Day"—but there are plenty of fun ones too!)

To capitalize on local news angles, create a calendar of major community events and anniversaries and pitch your story idea. Pitch lead times vary by outlet and format (print, broadcast, etc.)—but for a local story, one month of lead time should cover you.

USE ONLINE PITCH RESOURCES

Clearly, pitching effectively takes a lot of planning and effort. In between your strategic pitches, watch for opportunities for commentary and contributed pieces that may surface on sites like Help a Reporter Out (also called HARO, helpareporter.com) and Profnet.com. These sites exist to connect journalists with resources to help them build out stories for various publications.

These calls for contributions are usually very deadline oriented—so you'll need to keep your content matrix handy in order to pull from and adapt pieces you've already created (unless you are a tireless, speedy writer).

NEWSJACKING

The term *newsjacking* is a label given to the decades-old practice of attaching your publicity angle to a current event. Newsjacking is particularly effective via social media, where a company can respond almost instantaneously to outside news.

As an example, Oreo famously newsjacked the power outage during the 2013 Super Bowl at the New Orleans Superdome. Their Twitter post was a dark image of a single cookie with the caption "Power out? No problem. You can still dunk in the dark." This quick post earned thousands of retweets and shares. Humor works best with newsjacking, but organizations with products that can help solve problems or otherwise connect to current news can also benefit from this strategy.

Each of these angles provides an opportunity for you to get back into the spotlight. At a minimum, always issue a press release to be posted on your website pressroom and shared through distribution sites like Prlog. com to improve your discoverability and online presence. Or even better, have a plan in place to more fully capitalize on these events to get the most brand impact out of your hard-earned achievements.

As with any type of marketing, measuring the ROI (return on investment) of publicity can be a challenge. But with so many new products and services launching every day, can you really afford not to pursue it? Whether you tackle it on your own or hire a firm to help, a nice publicity hit can bring a surge of follow-on attention from other reporters to reward your efforts.

As you secure media placements, be sure to share those articles, interviews, speaking engagements, and the like. Keep a running list of your activities on your website, along with an updated press kit and speaking menu so people can easily identify you as an expert source for their topic.

Podcasts

According to a 2017 study by Edison Research, podcast listenership is on the rise, with monthly listeners growing from 21 to 24 percent year over year—and skewing toward an affluent, educated audience.[1]

Beyond watercooler favorites, many of the most popular podcasts fall into the categories of business, news, or self-help. They have become a place where listeners go to gain knowledge and grow. For experts and industry leaders, podcasts offer a unique experience to provide valuable, in-depth information to their audience. Beyond short-form content, like social media or blog posts, a podcast's long-form format allows you to cultivate a deeper relationship with your audience and grow your reach to new listeners at the same time.

Keynote and breakout-session content usually translates pretty directly into audio format, but books are a little different. You'll need to adjust your written content to include more stories and anecdotes to keep the listener engaged. Sound effects can also help keep your audience interested, but don't use them just for the sake of using them—they should add to the listener's experience or indicate transitions (à la the end-of-chapter chime).

If you're on the fence about starting a podcast, here are some reasons why you should consider it.

IT'S EASY

Let's get this point out of the way early. Starting a podcast sounds like a complicated venture, but in reality, it requires a minimal up-front investment and is surprisingly easy to implement. YouTube videos, like Pat Flynn's six-part guide to starting a podcast, break down all the steps to getting your own show up and running. There's no shortage of microphone reviews online to help you find the right microphone for your budget. Sites like Fiverr make developing the introductory music fast and inexpensive. By starting out with some thorough research, launching and continuing the recording process will not be the daunting process you may expect it to be.

---

1   "The Podcast Consumer 2017," Edison Research, April 18, 2017, http://www.edisonresearch.com/the-podcast-consumer-2017/.

IT ALLOWS YOU TO PRODUCE LONG-FORM CONTENT

In a world of information overload, we are bombarded with short-form content. Tweets, blog posts, news articles, and videos are meant to provide audiences with quick bursts of information and play a vital role in creating continued touch points between businesses and their audiences. But where blog posts and social media are limited to a few hundred words or characters, a podcast allows you to go deeper into your content.

According to Salesforce, "Three percent of monthly podcast consumers listen to the beginning of a podcast only. By and large, podcast listeners are loyal and committed to hearing out the full episode."[2] This means that there is an enormous opportunity here to showcase your expertise in a way that other formats can't accommodate. For businesses with complicated products or a long sales cycle, such in-depth content may allow consumers to make buying decisions more quickly.

YOU'RE SUPPORTING YOUR PARTNERS

The most common format for a podcast is an interview. As the host of your own show, bringing guests on to interview allows you not only to expand the information you're providing to your audience by tapping into your guest's expertise but also to support industry partners. By asking someone to be a guest on your show, you're giving them access to your audience, potentially helping your guest grow their reach. Likewise, if your guests promote the episode to their followers, you also tap into their audience. Both you and your guests can benefit from the added exposure, and by thinking of them as a guest, you may deepen your professional relationship with them as well. Just remember to structure your questions in a way that provides value to the listener so it doesn't come off as overly promotional.

YOU BUILD PERSONAL CONNECTION WITH YOUR AUDIENCE

Successful podcasts are rarely scripted and only lightly edited. As such, the host's personality has a chance to shine through in a seemingly

---

2   "20 Stats about the 2017 Podcast Consumer," Salesforce, April 25, 2017, https://
www.salesforce.com/blog/2017/04/20-stats-about-the-2017-podcast-consumer.html.

unfiltered way. Much like video, podcasts are one of the quickest ways to build personal connections and trust between a host and an audience. At a time when we have endless options for all of our purchasing decisions, trust is essential to building brand loyalty, and giving people a voice and a personality to connect to your brand helps to foster that trust.

IT PROVIDES A REPEAT TOUCH POINT FOR YOUR AUDIENCE

The value of a newsletter lies primarily in providing consistent content straight into your audience's inbox. Like a newsletter, when listeners subscribe to your podcast, they are agreeing to hear from you on a regular basis. The key is to stay consistent with your posting frequency and the kind of content you share. By doing so, your brand will stay top of mind, and you'll continue to develop trust and personal connection.

Luckily for you, the hardest part of making a podcast isn't on the technical side. The difficulty comes in cutting above the clutter and reaching your intended audience. To do so, it is vital that you provide quality content and execute your podcast in a way that is professional and compelling for people to listen to. Whether your intention is to put together a series or a one-time recording, a simple tool like an outline will help you gather your thoughts and verify that you are fulfilling the intention of what you want to say. The outline may also help you determine whether you have enough content for a series (or not).

For a list of helpful podcasting-creation, hosting, and promotion resources, visit the *Resources* section of ideasinfluenceandincome.com.

LAUNCH YOUR BOOK

After months—or, more likely, years—of thinking, writing, rethinking, and rewriting, you're within sight of your book's publication date and are dreaming about your name in lights, or maybe just on a few bookshelves here and there. And perhaps it will open some doors on the speaking front. As exhausted as you are after all of that writing, this is no time to rest. Your book launch is right around the corner, and it will take some considerable planning and strategizing to get the most out of it.

The success of your book's initial launch is important for a few reasons beyond celebrating the culmination of all your hard work. We've established that a book launch is a product launch, and product launches provide an angle to pitch the media and raise awareness of your ideas and message. A good book also gives the community of people you can reach through your platform something to talk about, which lies at the heart of creating word of mouth—the most powerful influence tool of all.

Finally, if retail distribution is a priority for you, it's important to understand that your book's sales figures during the first few months will most likely serve as a benchmark for its future distribution pattern. Retailers expect to see the most support around a book during the launch month, so if it doesn't do well then, they're unlikely to widen the distribution footprint from there. (Though, it's worth noting that I certainly have seen some exceptions to this.)

Timing is everything

Not understanding the timeline requirements for publicity and retail distribution is one of the most common mistakes authors make with book launches. Retail channels (airports, Barnes & Noble, indie chains, etc.) buy with at least five months' lead time, with that often stretching to eight months. It's important to adhere to that timeline so the book is being pitched when there's maximum budget to support its buy-in. So if your book is coming out in June, it may need to be pitched in January—and that means it needs to be pretty close to its final form in January too. Pitching late means pitching to a buyer with a much smaller budget to work with, which will lessen the opening retail buy.

Of course, if you're choosing to go the digital publishing route, the retail distribution timeline is irrelevant, since your book will only be retailed online. However, if you're still planning on a major media push to support your launch, bear in mind that "long-lead" print media and most book reviewers still operate with four to five months' lead time. Interview a couple of publicists early on to determine the type of campaign and channel strategy that might best suit your book and goals, then use that information to figure out the ideal release date. Your publicist may know of an event, holiday, or anniversary that could tie to your book for a strong media hook.

The preorder hustle

Once you've determined your publication date and publicity approach, it's time to start hustling sales. Many authors begin the hard work of generating sales for their book long before the actual release date. If you're a speaker, you have a unique opportunity to capture book sales (incorporated into your speaking fee) that can be leveraged during your launch. Gathering preorders for your book and running them through retail channels around your release date can add a nice boost to your opening sales numbers. There are a few options available here depending on your goals, your publishing model, and your priorities for the book launch.

One method for collecting preorders is to simply set up a preorder button on your book website that will prompt your customers to fill in their basic information and make a payment through your website for the books they order. It's also common to create a landing page specifically for preorders, which can be linked to from direct marketing pieces or inserts in newsletters. This is a popular option if you are incentivizing the customer's purchase via access to extra content or other downloadable incentives at no charge. Once the order is placed, the customer can be given a code to access all the promised free content and download directly from that page. Finally, collecting preorders can be as simple as keeping a spreadsheet with all of the order information you gather as you get your customers to place bulk orders leading up to the publication date.

A different option is to use a promotional blitz to send people directly to a retailer, such as Amazon, to place their orders during a specified period of time, usually immediately following the release of the book. In this case, it's important for your publisher or distributor to know how many orders you expect to be placed at least three weeks in advance so adequate stock can be moved into the supply chain to meet that rush of demand. This may also be your best option if you have sold your rights to a traditional publisher; in that scenario, you have less control over selling your books directly from your website.

Once you've collected your preorders, you'll need to determine the best fit for handling these sales. Have you gathered these preorders so you can generate maximum revenue from your book right away, or is your goal to have all of these sales count toward your retail track record? In hybrid publishing models like ours at Greenleaf Book Group, you have the flexibility to meet either goal. In a traditional publishing model, where you have sold your distribution rights, you'll need to confirm your options with your publisher before selling directly to one of your customers.

If you've accumulated a good number of preorders with a goal to drive your retail sales as high as they can go, you can run these sales through a retail channel so they are reported to BookScan and therefore become part of your auditable sales history. This is another time that BookScan can be useful. It serves as the best barometer of retail book sales through specific outlets that report such data. For bulk preorders, we often work with 800-CEO-READ (800ceoread.com)—a company that makes the direct sales process very simple. Your corporate customers can buy the books from 800-CEO-READ, which will directly bill your corporate customer for the sale. Then 800-CEO-READ will order the books from the publisher, who ships them directly to the customer, and finally will report the sales to BookScan. Barnes & Noble and Books-A-Million also have corporate buying programs to handle these types of orders.

Making a bestseller

To very loosely paraphrase the Bard, what's in a bestseller?

That which we call a *New York Times* bestseller by any other word (such as underground bestseller! Or Amazon bestseller!) would smell as sweet . . . well, not really.

As the number of books published each year continues to skyrocket, we face an onslaught of "bestseller" claims. We see it on marketing materials and press releases, on book covers and websites, and on the many submission forms that Greenleaf Book Group receives in its office each week. If this bestseller crown has not been awarded by one of the major publications, like *The New York Times*, *The Wall Street Journal*, or *USA Today*, is the publisher partaking in sensationalist marketing or just a stretch of the truth?

The short answer is that it depends on who the publisher is targeting with this information. If the publisher intends to woo the consumer with bestseller claims on the book cover, yes, there's some chance it could help. However, and this is a huge *however*, it could seriously hurt that publisher's reputation in the eyes of wholesalers, distributors, agents, and other parties within the closely knit publishing industry, and that harm could result in books not getting on shelves. Before you stretch the truth on a larger-than-life bestseller claim, be warned that you're not pulling the wool over the industry's eyes.

Industry types also have access to Nielsen's BookScan to research your sales history, and they will certainly consult them (among other resources) to corroborate your claims before making any decision to support your title. BookScan is a point-of-sale reporting service reflecting sales from approximately 70 percent of booksellers nationally. BookScan uses weekly data from over 6,500 retail, mass-merchant, and nontraditional outlets in combination with a statistical weighting methodology to present the most accurate information on sell-through available to the publishing industry. Certain notable accounts don't report, but regardless, BookScan is a strong barometer of sell-through and is very influential in how sales are measured and bestseller lists are compiled.

While BookScan offers great insights into overall sales numbers and trends, interestingly, it is not used exclusively (or sometimes at all) in building the prestigious bestseller lists. The holy grail of bestsellers lists is the one published by *The New York Times*. The methodology behind how this list is built is rather guarded and hush-hush. Most reports on the subject agree that *The New York Times* sends out a list of preselected trade titles (meaning titles you would find in a bookstore, not the boring academic titles like medical and law books that generally outsell them) to a selected group of close to 5,000 retailers and wholesalers for them to record weekly sales numbers on. There are allegedly blank lines for the recipients of this survey to write in titles not included on the form. That's a quaint thought, but from what I know about inventory managers, highly unlikely.

With any bestsellers list, it's important to note that it's a measurement of velocity of sales, not life of sales. A book that moves 5,000 copies in one week is likely to make some list in some capacity when that week's numbers are run; however, a book that sells 500 copies a week for ten weeks straight probably won't make any list at all. Lists also differ in how they categorize titles. For instance, *The New York Times* sorts by category (fiction, nonfiction, children's) and format (hardcover or trade paperback). On the other hand, *USA Today*'s list lumps them all together from 1 to 150 in sales numbers, period. This means that a book listed at number one on *The New York Times* hardcover fiction list could be ranking in the triple digits on the *USA Today* list.

Amazon's bestseller system is a separate beast that uses rankings without disclosing units sold. The rankings are recalculated hourly, which makes it rather easy to game. That said, while Amazon does not disclose its search algorithms, it is believed that achieving bestseller status helps a book's overall visibility and relevance in search results over the long term.

Differences in list building aside, the notable bestseller lists are meant as a barometer of American culture. No list is 100 percent accurate, and none purport to be. Still, bestseller status on a major list is highly coveted, highly profitable, and highly protected specifically so that the word *bestseller* does not become trite and meaningless. A thought leader who can legitimately claim their book is a bestseller enjoys a distinct point of differentiation because of it, which can in turn lead to more opportunities, higher speaking fees, and lucrative deals on any follow-up books.

Use your sales history to support your efforts to expand your publishing endeavors, but be wary of making unsubstantiated bestseller claims to influence industry types, who know very well that all that glitters is not gold.

Airport and front-of-store co-op placements

Imagine the thrill of walking through the airport, headed out on another business trip, and seeing your book staring back at you through the window of an airport bookstore. Or better yet, imagine reading an email from someone who bought your book in an airport bookstore or out of the window of their local retailer, read it, and then reached out to you to find out how to bring your message deeper into their organization through a speaking appearance or ongoing consulting arrangement. Close a deal like that, and your book pays for itself exponentially.

Whether in an airport or your local bookstore, premier shelf placement, face-out arrangement, and positioning on promotional stands (e.g., bookstore end caps, new release tables in the front of a store, and virtually all placements in airport bookstores) are paid for by publishers, distributors, and authors. It's ridiculously valuable real estate due to high traffic and visibility, and in the case of airports, you can add excellent buyer demographics to that mix. It's not extortion for retailers to ask for payment to place your titles in these premium positions. It's capitalism, and it happens at all levels of retail.

So does this mean that any author—regardless of the quality of their work—can pay their way into the most trafficked areas of bookstores? Are we being fed content based on riches instead of richness?

In a word: no.

Authors cannot simply walk into Barnes & Noble's corporate headquarters with a check for $20,000 and demand premier placement across the country. Though publishers, distributors, and authors do pay for the placement, retailers are very selective about which books receive the opportunity for promotion. The buyers who select the titles in these placements are evaluated on sell-through performance. Yes, an author or publisher has to pay to get that space, but since everybody wants it, the retailer will select the product that they believe will move the most units.

Long story short, they base their decisions on sales potential, which boils down to—

- Author's platform and name recognition
- Cover design
- Quality of content
- Author's marketing plan

If you want this premier store placement for your book, you will need—

- All of the items listed above
- A publisher or distributor with a strong history of negotiating co-op promotions
- Six months of lead time to pitch a mostly final product

So how does a book end up on the new release table at an airport's entrance or the "New Year, New You" display at the front of Barnes & Noble? Here's a quick breakdown of the process.

First, the publisher or distributor's sales rep meets with the category buyer. The reps generally pitch buyers five to six months in advance of publication and, by that time, already have dust jackets, galleys, blads or review copies, and marketing plans to add weight to the pitch. Each rep must have at least five titles in the category in order to get a meeting with the buyer, so note that sales reps are not self-published authors with no distributor. The reps meet with the buyers at the retail outlet (if independent) or the corporate headquarters (if a chain). Unless the retailer is a small independent, store employees and floor managers do not decide on what books to carry or promote, so do not waste your time pounding the pavement. (Exception: Some stores will support local authors with small displays purchased on a consignment basis, but in general, placement decisions are made by buyers, not managers or clerks.)

Then the rep solicits a buy and a placement promotion if co-op money is available. Co-op is what the retailers call *placement promotions*. The term comes from *cooperative advertising*, stemming from the major publishing houses' practice of allocating a set percentage of the previous year's sales for co-op to be divvied out between titles as agreed upon by the publisher and bookseller. After the sales rep finishes pitching a book, the buyer typically informs the rep how many copies that particular retailer will likely carry when the book comes off the press.

If the publisher, distributor, or author has a budget for co-op promotions, the rep negotiates the placement directly with the buyer. The buyer will only offer a co-op placement for the book that he or she believes will sell the most copies in that space at that time. At the risk of beating a dead horse, Retail 101: location, location, location. Buyers will not sell the best real estate in their store to a title that won't perform. If Dr. Oz's newest diet book about some magical, exotic super fruit will outsell your book of poetry on the front-of-store table, it is not likely that the space will be available to you.

After that, if the title performs well, the rep may be able to negotiate an extension. Bookstore co-op placements are usually sold in blocks of two to four weeks. Airport placements are sold in month-long blocks or longer. If the book sells well during that time, reps can try to negotiate extensions, though even the strongest seller may be locked out if there's no unpurchased space available. Extensions are based on sell-through and available space. If a book sells well, the space is available, and the retailer believes the demand will be sustained for a notable period of time, they may offer to extend the promotion. Time consumer-marketing efforts like publicity to coincide with your co-op promotions. If you do not drive consumers into stores while the book has the premier spot, your book will be returned once the placement expires.

Launch redux

Fast-forward to one month after your book's release date. Hopefully, all of your careful planning and hard work have paid off with strong opening sales numbers. But what if your publicity is falling flat or the book is just not selling well through retail channels?

The good news is that the proverbial ship has not completely sailed. While it's certainly true in the media business that many products just don't find an audience, I'd argue that the issue is typically one of positioning or lack of platform rather than bad content. Are you gracefully working the title of your book into your interviews? Many authors are used as experts on national news programs and never mention the title of their book. Is there a national news event or trend that you can creatively piggyback to bring attention to your message? Have you made full use of video and social media? If the audience you've been targeting is not responding, is there a secondary audience you can target with a revised pitch? For instance, a book on resilience with a primary audience of leaders could be retargeted to serve single parents, people with chronic diseases, victims of violent crime, and so on.

If you have an ebook and can control its pricing, this may be a good time to experiment with temporary free or $0.99 price points to make it easy for readers to take a chance on your content. Very often, a spike in discounted ebooks translates to a spike in print sales as positive reviews and higher sales boost online visibility.

MAINTAIN YOUR AUDIENCE AFTER THE LAUNCH

The launch of a book, or any product, can earn a lot of attention from the media, industry colleagues, and the public in general. Debut launches done right are sexy and full of potential, bringing with them opportunities for feature stories, author profiles, "ones to watch" lists, and so on.

After the shiny launch veneer has worn off, how do you remain on the radar of the influencers who can help your brand grow?

The good news is that every reader you acquired during your book launch now adds to your invaluable "platform" of people interested in your message. Now, be smart about keeping them in your community. This doesn't have to be overwhelming—keep it simple. At the end of your book, include a page encouraging the reader to sign up for free tools and exclusive content via your website. Once a quarter, share something of value with them, such as speaking videos, infographics, white papers, and audio downloads. The more exclusive this content is, the better; people love to feel special. This will help sustain valuable word-of-mouth momentum and awareness with your audience while simultaneously building your list.

After all, you'll need that list to make all of this easier with the launch of your next book, right?

In today's economy, your customers (readers) are your audience. In addition to supporting you by buying your books, they follow your Twitter account, like your Instagram photos, and share your posts on LinkedIn.

With the growth of social media, customers themselves have become a marketing opportunity—and they base their first impressions of a brand largely on the quality of its social media content. Social media is also an efficient and economical way to keep your audience close after your initial point of engagement.

To revisit our previous discussion of social media, though most authors use social media in some form, many don't realize that it's not enough just to gain legions of followers. If you have 100,000 followers on your company's Twitter, LinkedIn, newsletter, and the like but never update these channels, or if you bombard followers with advertisements, you'll see your audience decline as quickly as it grew.

The key to maintaining an audience on (and off) social media is to regularly meet your followers where they are. Here are a few ways to do that.

Know them

Much like stand-up comedians read a room to know what their audience finds funny, authors and experts should read social media trends and articles written by members of their audience to hone in on the needs and interests of their readers. Do they value luxury? Are they looking for advice or humor? Are they drawn to brands with a higher purpose?

When executing any marketing strategy, know what story you want to tell and for whom it is intended. This is another area where creating audience personas—a detailed bio of your target reader—can help you set the appropriate tone for your content.

Having a clear storyline to follow for a clear audience will help ensure that your social media content is compelling long after you first make contact with someone, even if someone else on your team handles your social media.

Give to get

Like any strong relationship, your interaction with your audience should be mutually beneficial.

Every time you post on social media, ask yourself what your audience is getting out of it. It could be a link to a helpful article related to your industry, a free ebook download, a product or service giveaway, or an announcement about an upcoming exclusive event that your audience would love. Make sure what you're offering your audience is worth their time, or they'll stop spending time on you at all. The 80/20 rule of 80 percent engagement, 20 percent promotion is a solid benchmark to strike the right balance here.

Show up

Brand loyalty is a huge factor in your company's success, and it's built on trust. Customers don't grow to trust a brand that they rarely see or one that doesn't convey a clear personality, so be consistent and transparent with your followers.

If you haven't already (and you should have), create an editorial calendar for your social media to plan what (and when) you'll be posting on your company's channels. Content doesn't need to be added every day on every channel, but it does need to be added consistently. As customers learn that there will be something new and interesting coming from you regularly, they'll be more inclined to continue following and sharing your posts.

Gestures of appreciation are also important ways to reinforce your connection with your audience, both online and offline. Whether it's through a handwritten note or a direct message online, scheduling in some routine, personalized, one-on-one thanks will earn an abundance of goodwill.

Social media has made it more important than ever to value your audience and to make it enjoyable for them to interact with you. If you listen to them and actively strive to meet them where they are, you'll see your audience continue to grow in size and loyalty well beyond your book launch.

In terms of angles you can use to breathe new life into an old book, look for hallmark events and achievements, like anniversaries and major milestones, that might grab the attention of the press.

ANNIVERSARIES

New product launches come and go at a rapid-fire pace, so mark and celebrate meaningful anniversaries to bring attention to your staying power and long-term growth. Incremental five-year anniversary marks are most common—for instance, your book's five-year anniversary, ten-year anniversary, and so on.

You can also use your anniversary as an opportunity to reach out to valued partners with a commemorative gift to make a follow-up impression and to acknowledge their role in your progress.

MAJOR MILESTONES

Longevity is certainly not the only (or best) measurement of success. Take stock of the major milestones that impact your brand, and designate someone to monitor your progress toward them so you can publicize accordingly when you reach those meaningful marks.

For instance, you might celebrate your 1,000th review, a certain number of units sold, x number of ebook downloads, or a target book sales revenue mark. How you celebrate depends on your culture and your budget. At a minimum, do a press release and post it in the pressroom section of your website. Big spender? Sponsor a party at an event like SXSW, and invite all of the important people who should be talking about you.

Lift off

The idea of launching your book into the world may seem like a daunting task, but if you're prepared and know what to expect, it doesn't have to be. Use your already-established brand and platform to help your chances of successful publication, and then be diligent and committed to keeping your book top of mind for your readers.

Just reading about all of this ongoing work may exhaust you. Take heart in the fact that—while the launch itself will require your direct participation for media interviews, speaking engagements, and so on—much of the follow-up work can be hired out or delegated to someone on your staff, with your general oversight.

Overall, there's no getting around the fact that creating influence requires a lot of hustle. If it were easy, everybody would be an influencer. If you're serious about establishing thought leader status, take the time to set up the systems and strategies described in this section before your book launch. As with any product launch, planning and execution will make or break you.

PART 3

$

INCOME

Chapter 11

OPTIONS FOR PUBLISHING

*An author who gives a manager or publisher any rights in his work
except those immediately and specifically required for its publication
or performance is for business purposes an imbecile.*
—George Bernard Shaw

TODAY'S PUBLISHING LANDSCAPE BRINGS a wide range of partners, business models, and brands for an author to consider. The evolution of our industry has placed more power in authors' hands than ever. And as we learned from Spider-Man, with great power comes great responsibility. Choosing the right publishing option for your book can make the difference between a successful launch with a high-quality book or a retail bomb that reflects poorly on your brand.

Each publishing option also has implications on your control over certain rights to your work and, therefore, affects your ability to independently repurpose and monetize your content. We touched on the different publishing models briefly in Chapter 1, but we'll go into deeper detail in this chapter. Let's take a look at how each of the major options shakes out.

TRADITIONAL PUBLISHING

In a traditional publishing deal, an acquisitions editor representing the publisher will negotiate a deal with the author's agent. While terms vary from project to project, first-time authors usually receive an advance on royalties of $2,000 to $20,000.

Once the publisher sells enough books that the total royalties (not total sales) earn out the advance, the author begins receiving royalties beyond the advance, which range anywhere from 5 to 7 percent for paperback and 10 to 15 percent for hardcover books. (Remember—the agent is also taking 10–15 percent off the top of the author's royalties.)

For authors who are thought leaders or consultants (or value keeping control over their work for other reasons), the ownership of certain rights should be a major consideration in the publishing option decision-making process. Under the traditional model, authors sell the right to publish their work for a defined period of time. Since the publisher bears the risk in this deal, the author typically has little say in the creative direction, distribution, or length of time their book is championed in the retail marketplace.

The specific rights held by the publisher vary from contract to contract and may also include film rights, audiobook rights, foreign translation rights, workshop rights, and rights to ancillary materials. The more rights the publisher holds, the better they are set up to recoup their investment in the book. Of course, the other side of that coin is that it leaves authors with fewer ways to directly monetize their own content.

Given that the publisher has acquired the publishing rights and is investing in the production of the books in this scenario, they own the actual inventory of books. In most cases, authors who sell directly to an audience (if their contract allows for this) through speaking engagements, corporate consulting, and so on must buy their books back from the publisher before selling them to their corporate clientele. This is separate from a *buyback clause*, which is a mandatory purchase of books from the publisher made by the author at a contractually stated price and quantity. Publishers often use buyback clauses to help cover their expense and reduce risk on projects with limited or unknown sales potential.

And yes, sometimes the buyback cancels out the advance.

SELF-PUBLISHING

Despite the allure of traditional publishing for many authors, quite often, self-publishing is an appropriate option to bring a book to market. On top of being the fastest way to market and often the most cost effective, it offers authors the most control.

Self-publishing has brought about the democratization of publishing. For centuries, agents and publishers tightly controlled the selection of manuscripts to be published. But with the introduction of technology-enabled, scalable platforms to help authors publish and make their work available, today every author can be published with the click of a button.

In many ways, this is a good thing. Authors once rejected because they served too small of a market (often the most disenfranchised voices) now have a way to share their work regardless of whether a media conglomerate can profit from it. Today, the majority of new titles published each year arrive to market via self-publishing.

The downside of this swell of self-published work lies in the inevitable poor quality and low sales of a book that is produced without professional guidance. While there are exceptions, most self-published titles cannot compete with the quality of the books being released by established, reputable publishers. To write a book is hard enough; many self-published authors task themselves with being writers, editors, designers, project coordinators, marketers, and sales managers. That's a tall order that often comes up short.

This has resulted in an access problem for self-published authors. As one example, mainstream reviewers rarely give coverage to self-published works alongside traditional books. They generally offer reviews to these authors for a fee in a separate section of their publication. They simply don't have the resources to sift through the haystack, looking for the proverbial needle.

Hands down, the biggest roadblock that self-published authors hit is access to retail distribution. Retailers are not equipped to deal with the administrative load of setting up a single-title publisher as a vendor or dealing with the associated carrying costs of dealing with low-margin partners. For that reason, they often close the door in the face of the self-published author and tell them to find a distributor to represent their book. Distributors, in turn, are selective because they work on micro-margins and rely on volume to turn a profit. This leaves many self-publishers to depend completely on online sales (which is not necessarily a deal breaker since, depending on your genre, that averages upward of 50 percent of the market for a given book). So self-publishing may not be right for everyone—in many cases, a hybrid model is the best fit.

HYBRID PUBLISHING

Hybrid models exist in different iterations, all with varying business models and terms, but most of them intend to bridge self-publishing and traditional publishing. The most successful hybrid publishers maintain a level of selectivity and quality that competes with their traditional brethren in order to access brick-and-mortar retail markets.

Greenleaf Book Group, for instance, has built its model around providing authors with all of the advantages of self-publishing (speed to market, ownership of rights, creative control, and high royalties) combined with the expertise and distribution muscle you'd find with a traditional publisher—a position we enjoy by virtue of starting as a distributor and developing our titles based on market feedback.

Since most hybrid models allow authors to retain their rights, the risk model is flipped from the traditional approach. The author keeps the lion's share of the book sales margin and the revenue from ancillary rights, like film, foreign translations, workshops, and so on. That stronger upside requires more front-end investment from the author since the publisher keeps less revenue from these channels, so a hybrid approach best suits the confident writer who is comfortable putting some skin in the game.

Similar to self-publishing, the author who publishes in a hybrid model usually enjoys control and flexibility of revenue streams that fall outside of trade book sales. Unlike self-publishing, the hybrid author will have a stronger support system and a known industry brand to help create a competitive product and open doors that would otherwise remain closed.

To recap, here are five key points to consider as you research the best publishing business model for your book.

Consider the ownership of rights

When dealing with traditional publishers, you don't sell them ownership of the book itself but rather the right to reproduce and sell your work. So long as they own those rights, the publishing house has control over how your book is published, how it is packaged, and when it is delivered. In contrast, self-publishing allows you to retain all rights and ownership of your work, as well as control over the creative direction and distribution of your work. Many hybrid options involving author investment also allow the author to retain rights and ownership while granting access to quality workmanship and distribution.

Examine potential sales channels and payout

On a royalties basis, self-publishing provides the highest returns. Authors generally receive 20–35 percent of the cover price for books sold through retailers and 100 percent of the retail price for all books sold directly from the author to the consumer.

Traditional publishing contracts typically pay out 5–15 percent of the cover price, and that's only after money paid as an advance on royalties is recovered through retail sales. However, traditional distribution models may bring much larger volume of sales than self-published authors can accomplish alone.

Hybrid models provide easy access to online sales plus the distribution muscle required to sell in the brick-and-mortar landscape, but they generally do not pay a significant advance (if any) and often require a fee in exchange for publishing services.

Determine the importance of time to market

Between developing a proposal, finding an agent, and working through the publishing process, traditional publishing can require years to go from idea to finished product on the shelves.

Self-publishing lets you get to market in a fraction of that time. For timely subjects like technology and politics, this is a major plus.

Traditional publishers and hybrid models with strong brick-and-mortar distribution programs will need a certain amount of lead time as dictated by retail buyers' merchandising calendars. The retail buying schedules (for Barnes & Noble, airport accounts, etc.) still require at least five months' lead time, meaning they need to be pitched with a fairly robust picture of the book to come and its related marketing campaign that far ahead of the publication date to earn interest and shelf-space commitment.

Due to how buying budgets are allocated at the retail level, abiding by merchandising timelines can have major implications on your book's rollout (or lack thereof). So avoid unnecessary and rushed "shotgun publishing" if retail bookstore and airport distribution are among your goals.

Understand the importance of quality

To reiterate, self-publishing as a whole is not known for its quality of product. Retailers often refuse to carry self-published books because they fall short of the retailer's standards for strong content, design, and sales potential.

However, there are a few standout companies producing high-caliber self-published materials that either meet or exceed industry standards. Compare the quality of a prospective self-publisher's produced materials with those available through national retailers before committing to a partner. Also ask other industry professionals to evaluate the self-publisher's work since they will have a stronger grasp on industry standards and quality measures.

Hybrid publishers who have a track record for selling into retail accounts probably have strong quality standards. Any publisher who does not present quality material to retail buyers won't be selling books to them for long. A publisher's history of awards, bestsellers, strong reviews, and similar accolades can all help to confirm a reputation for quality. Many companies claim to be customer centric with a commitment to quality, but the proof is often found in what others are saying.

Traditional publishers are assumed to have strong quality standards, and with established publishing houses, that's typically true. Just remember that in this model, creative control remains with the publisher because they are funding the book's production—so you may have to be more vocal about your design or content preferences, and be prepared to possibly not get your way.

Remember, this is your hard-earned brand that you're putting out there, and it's hard to pull back once it's live.

Assess your risk tolerance and investment capability

In exchange for the author's higher royalties and retention of rights found in self-publishing and hybrid models, you will typically find a larger author-funded upfront investment. Here, the author typically assumes the risk for publishing, covering elements of production that can include editing, design, printing, shipping, and warehousing.

In business terms, it's similar to comparing bootstrapping to venture capital. The party bearing the risk (making the investment) reaps greater rewards on the backend.

When considering cost risks, keep in mind that authors are almost always responsible for the bulk of their own publicity costs, whether publishing through a traditional house or as a self-publisher. Your publisher may incorporate some marketing efforts to promote the book to the industry, reviewers, and communities of readers, but unless you're Stephen King, you'll be funding your own general publicity campaign.

Another risk revolves around control of your book's longevity. Traditional publishing requires no initial investment from the author to cover publishing costs, but if sales are poor, traditional publishers may move it to a digital-only edition or otherwise limit its retail availability, tying up your content until the contractual publishing rights revert to you or are bought back.

DIGITAL PUBLISHING

For most publishers, digital publishing lives alongside print. It's not an either-or equation. Looking back across media, there are quite a few examples of new formats threatening the old . . . and then coexisting. TV was a big threat to radio. Cable TV and VHS home movies were a threat to movie theaters—as was Netflix. Ultimately, each provides a different experience. That is the key to successful digital publishing—to maximize the experience that the format allows.

As far as exposure to an audience, there's a push-pull balance that has always been around in publishing. For a long while, publishing successes were dictated by what the traditional publishers "pushed" out onto the finite shelf space of brick-and-mortar bookstores. If the public liked the book, "pull" (demand) followed, and sell-through was strong, reprints ensued. If pull was not strong, the books went to the shredder and that was that. Digital publishing, and the spread of opinions online, is swaying the balance toward pull.

Like technology so often does, this democratizes the business of getting your book out to the world. You're not reliant on publishers and retailers to get your book to the reading public. You can publish and promote online, build an auditable sales history, and leverage that for more favorable publishing terms later.

So the question is not whether to include digital publishing in your publishing strategy but rather how to get the most out of the options available to you.

It's especially important for a new author to understand what digital publishing can and cannot do in terms of retail reach.

In this context, *digital publishing* means making a book available through ebook and print-on-demand formats. Ebooks are downloaded and read on electronic devices. Print-on-demand books exist as a digital file until someone orders a copy, at which point that specific order is printed on demand.

Ebooks

As one publishing option, ebook-only publishers offer services at a low cost with fast speed to market. However, most ebook publishers accept manuscripts as vanity publishers do—based on few or no editorial criteria. Without being able to judge a book by production value or publisher, buyers, reviewers, and the media have no reliable way to assess quality and will likely pass on media coverage or retail commitment.

When looking at the numbers from a year-over-year growth curve, ebooks initially experienced dramatic growth as various iterations of e-readers, tablets, and ebook reading apps evolved to serve readers with a preference for this new format. The perks of fast and easy download and lower pricing are alluring for passionate readers, assuming they don't mind losing the tactile experience of holding a book.

That said, ebook sales as a percentage of overall book sales have slipped enough in the past few years to assure most industry analysts that publishing is not destined to mirror the recording industry in terms of complete digital transformation.[1]

With ebooks comprising roughly 10–20 percent of sales, depending on genre, most publishers offer them alongside a print version of the book, whether that print version is made available through print-on-demand or traditional offset printing and distribution into bookstores. Publishing in multiple formats maximizes a publisher's means of reaching readers.

Print-on-demand

Digital publishing is an evolving area that offers authors additional options. Typically, a digital publisher chooses to release new projects exclusively in ebook and print-on-demand (POD) formats.

POD is widely marketed as a profitable alternative to traditional printing and publishing. It's important to note that there is a difference between POD printers and POD publishers. POD publishers typically

---

1 Alexandra Alter, "The Plot Twist: E-Book Sales Slip, and Print Is Far from Dead," *The New York Times*, September 22, 2015, https://www.nytimes.com/2015/09/23/business/media/the-plot-twist-e-book-sales-slip-and-print-is-far-from-dead.html.

offer basic file preparation, design, and editorial services. After providing these services, POD publishers use a POD printer to produce books and make them available online and by special order in bookstores. You can use a POD publisher as a middleman and service provider, or you can work directly with a POD printer. When deciding whether to move forward with a POD publishing option, consider the following:

- Like many ebook publishers, most POD publishers accept projects regardless of quality. This association can result in negative stigma and reactions from media and the book industry.

- For the most part, POD titles are not actively stocked in bookstores. Typically, if consumers want a particular POD title, they have to order it from a bookstore or online. This makes it a good option for authors focused on online promotion.

- Few consumers special order books from bookstores; most commonly, they buy a book that is already in stock, or they order from their favorite online retailer.

- When working with certain POD publishers, you may pay for an interior layout and cover design but may not own the rights to the formatted files. In other words, if you leave your publisher (or freelance contractor) for a new publisher, you may not be given the application files or high-resolution files you need and will thus have to pay a second time to have the interior manuscript formatted and the cover designed.

Unlike POD publishers, POD printers typically do not offer design, editorial, or other publishing services, but they can be extremely valuable resources, particularly when printing books with unknown or limited sales potential.

If you need a few copies in a rush, good POD printers can offer unmatched turnaround times. If you are seeking a national book release, however, you should consider the following:

- If you expect to sell more than a thousand copies, your production price per unit will be notably lower if you use a traditional offset printer.

- POD printers do not offer as many technology and feature options as offset printers, so your design and manufacturing options will be limited to very basic specifications.

- The main issue to consider with digital options is whether they offer you the optimal chance of success in your particular market. Many publishers (including Greenleaf Book Group) use digital publishing options for projects with niche or focused markets and to complement standard formats but generally recommend traditional printing and sales channels for authors and publishers seeking mass distribution.

- Shipping and warehousing is something else to consider—with traditional offset printing, you'll need a place to store your books, and you may have shipping costs to cover, depending on your terms. With POD distribution, everything is digital, so these carrying costs are mitigated.

- Print-on-demand technology has advanced quickly, but most POD resources still have limitations around nonstandard formats and design effects.

- POD and digital printers have a quicker turnaround time, usually about two weeks, whereas offset printing usually requires four to five weeks for paperback and six to eight weeks for hardcover.

Now that you have a basic understanding of the options available and their respective pros and cons, you'll need to evaluate your skills, goals, project, and budget to determine which approach is best for you.

Regardless of which option you choose to pursue, it is vital that you protect yourself by doing your homework, taking the time to weigh the pros and cons, and analyzing each option's ability to help you meet your short- and long-term goals.

Publishing a book is a smart and crucial step toward building your brand. While there are many ways to publish your book, there is not necessarily a right or a wrong approach. Each author has different goals, resources, content, and even commitment level. Take the time to carefully consider your publishing priorities to ensure your path to market is well aligned with your objectives as an author.

SUPPOSE YOUR BOOK DOESN'T SELL

Ever wonder what happens to the unsold books sitting in the major publishers' warehouses across the country once that publisher decides to call it quits on a title?

One of the quirks about the publishing industry is that books are bought on a returnable basis. That means they are not sold until they are sold to both the retailer *and* the end user. Short term, if a book doesn't sell through brick-and-mortar channels in sixty days or less, it is sent back to the publisher or distributor. That creates a return, which undoes the sale for all involved and essentially makes publishing a consignment business.

Long term, this practice transfers most of the risk to the publisher or distributor since the retailer can wipe their hands clean of inventory at the first sign of slow performance. This is good in the sense that it removes some of the risk for retailers to take a chance on an unproven product, but it's bad in terms of the extra pressure on an author to create enough demand to move the supply chain inventory before those books are turned around and sent back home, with handling-damaged covers and tails between their legs, to their publisher's warehouse.

In short, an underperforming book gets the hook. This hook isn't the one that a roomful of people spend weeks devising to convince the media and public to pay attention to the title in the first place; it's the one that unceremoniously pulls our featured performer offstage.

In the interest of making sense of all of this, let's clarify the difference between *books* and *titles*. In the publishing industry, a *title* refers to an individual work of intellectual property. *Books* refers to multiple reproductions of the *title*. So we may say that a certain *title* has 20,000 *books* in print.

Publishing is as unpredictable as the tastes of its master, the public. If any publisher knew the secret formula to a locked-in bestseller at the consumer level, he or she would be a gazillionaire. The reality is that creators of media are at the mercy of a lot of factors beyond their control.

A publisher may look at a potential new addition to their line and consider the quality of the work, the performance of comparable titles (*comp titles,* in industry speak), the author's platform, marketing budget, initial feedback from sales reps, and the current buzz on the subject matter to determine whether or not to take the plunge on a new title. If all signs say go, the publisher engages their editorial staff for improvements, finalizes a marketing strategy, solicits buy estimates from excited sales reps, and goes to press for a significant quantity of books. So far, so good.

Unfortunately, the public and the marketplace can be fickle. Public opinion on the subject of a biography or an issue may turn, an unexpected competing title may be issued around the same time, or the title just may never hit with the media or the public. It's a guessing game to some degree, and we all guess incorrectly here and there.

When a publisher has a surplus of inventory and a lack of sales momentum, remaindering the books is an option to at least recover a portion of production costs. Remainders are overstock units of a title that may be sold in large quantities through a bid list to bargain book wholesalers. The wholesalers then resell them to retailers. These books may also be sold directly to retailers in smaller quantities in what is referred to as a *white sale.* In general, remainders bids come in at less than 10 percent of retail price under an exclusive buy arrangement. The market skews heavily toward the soccer mom demographic—gardening, travel, cooking, lifestyle, and parenting. A remaindered title will generally be taken out of print or have its barcode punched in an effort to safeguard against returns to wholesalers and retailers at the full price.

When making a decision on how to proceed in publishing your title, this information is important in a couple of ways. First, to give your title more time to sell, consider holding on to your distribution rights and publishing outside of the major houses so that you may have more control over how long your title stays in print. Second, remember that it's a crowded marketplace. Hone the value, uniqueness, and quality of your product, and invest in marketing support. You've got a lot of competition. Third, realize that these remaindered titles are competing on the same turf as your new book at a fraction of your cover price, and then *reread the second point.*

Do your homework and plan carefully up front to give your title its best shot at a successful launch and a long, profitable backlist life.

Understand your options

Choosing a publishing option that works for your priorities and goals is important in order to keep the book side of your content machine humming without interruption. Going through the process of trying to get a reversion of rights from a traditional publisher so you can self-publish can take considerable time and can create lapses in your book's retail availability. Going in the other direction, self-publishing and then deciding to pursue a traditional deal to access wider distribution, can be a challenge if your book did not initially perform well (although these deals certainly do happen).

Regardless, you do have options to move around the industry. Depending on the way your deal is structured, it just may take you some time to exit one arrangement and move into the next if you're unhappy with the model you chose. Authors are increasingly choosing to move around the publishing industry from project to project, releasing subsequent titles in the business model that makes the most sense for their book at that time.

As you explore the various publishing options available, including digital models, it's worth noting the approaches and partners that intrigue you so you can more easily begin those conversations should you decide to write more books. (For what it's worth, the authors I work with who have written multiple books swear that it gets a bit easier each time.)

Chapter 12

BUILDING BLOCKS: PRODUCTIZING YOUR WRITING

A market is never saturated with a good product,
but it is very quickly saturated with a bad one.
—Henry Ford

AFTER MANY YEARS WORKING WITH THOUGHT LEADERS developing books, I've noticed a curious trend related to their content: They often don't think they have much. Of course, after a bit of prodding, they are inevitably able to inventory an impressive range of material ranging from presentations to video and accumulated stories they've tucked away for possible use down the road. Some ideas aren't really big enough for a book but might make an interesting blog post or magazine article. Other ideas are too much for one book and need to be broken down into clearer, more confined subject areas. Suddenly, they have the opposite problem from the one they originally thought they had—lots of different content and no idea how to strategically put it to work to build a message, an audience, and a brand.

If you're in this category, fear not—we have a process for evaluating these different ideas and content assets to determine their best, most effective use.

CREATE A CONTENT INVENTORY

After you've whittled your content down to the good, current material that supports your goals, loosely organize it by length. As a basic guideline, consider anything under 1,000 words (under two minutes for audio or video) as short-form content; 1,000–40,000 words (under ten minutes for audio or video) as medium-form content; and over 40,000 words (over ten minutes for audio or video) as long-form content. These length guidelines are really "time required to consume" guidelines that will help you determine the best outlets for each content piece. Blog readers expect quick, succinct pieces (the short-form category), whereas a book reader is prepared to give you hours of his or her time.

Short-form content

Short-form content, like social media activity, blog posts, and short videos, provides a great opportunity to test ideas, particularly if you aren't completely clear on what your audience wants to hear. As you blog and interact with your community, take note of which topics or hooks are most commented on, shared, and liked. Over time, you will see a trend that will help guide your overall messaging. This category is also where a lot of the ongoing engagement so critical to building a community occurs. Short-form content keeps you on the radar in between the release of medium- and long-format pieces.

Medium-form content

Medium-form content, like shorter ebooks, articles, video tutorials, white papers, and so on, often makes up the bulk of your assets. While audiences generally expect short-form content to be free and long-form content to be paid, the medium-form group is a gray idea ripe with opportunity and ready for creativity. If your driving goal is to drive brand awareness or build a list, these medium-form assets are great tools to leverage for promotions and newsletter sign-ups. Greenleaf Book Group author Melissa Rodriguez did a great job of this with the release of her book on hearing loss, *Hear Your Life*, which uses inspirational stories to help the hearing impaired and their families deal with the devastating effects of hearing loss. The book directs readers to Melissa's website for additional resources, where exclusive content downloads are available to three strategically targeted audiences: individuals with hearing loss, loved ones of those with hearing loss, and physicians and healthcare providers. Melissa was more interested in helping people and spreading brand awareness, so she chose to make these available without a sign-up wall. If list building was more important to her, readers would have to sign up for a newsletter before being able to access this high-value content specific to their own lives and situations.

Medium-form content is also great for promotional purposes or to bundle and sell as a combined product. For example, a business author with multiple articles, a short ebook, and a video on improving sales performance can bundle these together and use them as a giveaway to drive sign-ups, a bonus for audience members at a speaking engagement, an incentive to preorder an upcoming book release, or a standalone product. Resist the temptation to include content not aligned with your goals or message into this category. Everything you put out into the world leaves a permanent record, and it all contributes to your brand and how your audience perceives you.

Long-form content

The most obvious long-form format is a book (video can fall into this group too). It's essential to work with a good editor to ensure your book will be over 60,000 words in length, which is the standard minimum word count for a general trade release (there are exceptions, of course, but 60,000 words is a solid benchmark). If you're throwing filler into the manuscript to beef it up, it may be time to take a step back and consider whether that topic might be more appropriate in medium-form length, perhaps as an article, a white paper, or a Kindle Single (Amazon's dedicated storefront for shorter works). On the other end of that spectrum, if you have to cut material from the book for the sake of length, consider whether that material might have another home somewhere else in your content strategy. For example, a case study that was removed for length could be the basis of a white paper supporting your services.

As we learned in the *Ideas* section, the rules around a book's length largely exist for books intended for retail bookstore distribution, due to merchandising concerns (your book needs to be long enough to have some presence on the shelf when it's positioned spine out) and sales modeling systems. If you choose to forego that publishing model and opt for a print-on-demand or other digital release, the rules around length ease up.

One caveat to remember when we're talking about all types and all lengths of content is that—whether we're talking about content in the form of a print book, an ebook, a white paper, a blog, the speaking platform, Twitter, Facebook, or anything else—content provides tools for conversation and engagement, not a substitute. The best brands build conversation (and thus create influence) around great ideas. Once you've clarified your goals and messaging, you'll find it much easier to create strategic, impactful content that consistently supports your brand moving forward.

MONETIZE YOUR MESSAGE

For speakers and writers, content is king, or so the saying goes—but building a kingdom can be incredibly time-consuming, potentially pulling you away from promoting your services to your core audience and creating even more hats for you to wear as you grow your speaking business. Leveraging content across multiple platforms is a no-brainer in terms of expanding both revenue and reach, but doing it right requires a fair amount of forethought and intent. So how do you use your existing content to create more value for your audience? Is using that content to create useful supplementary products an option?

Our editors at Greenleaf Book Group are trained to think beyond the "bookstore" book and innovate ways of applying content in new formats that help authors and speakers monetize their message across multiple types of audiences. Pulling from these editors' years of experience, we've put together some pointers that will help you best approach presenting your content in new structures—what we call *ancillary materials*—and leverage them to capture, and create more value for, your target markets.

The benefits of ancillary materials like reading guides, webinars, book summaries, and workbooks are many.

Ancillary materials are an obvious way to leverage and monetize the content you've already created. They allow you to target your material toward key customer channels, create custom content for individual clients, and give your existing customers additional products to buy. For speakers, a diverse product base is critical for creating scalable revenue and buzz that outlasts the standing ovation.

Beyond the obvious revenue benefits, ancillary materials should also be leveraged as powerful audience-capture tools on the marketing side of your business. If a reader picks up your book at an airport, reads it, and loves it, ideally, that person will hire you to speak to or consult with their organization to help them implement the methods or changes advocated in your book. It's great when that happens, but realistically, the majority of readers may not immediately take that step. That's why it's imperative that you position ancillary materials in a way to best help you convert passive readers into active leads. For instance, at the back of a book on business leadership, you can entice the reader to visit your website for exclusive content available to readers who enter a specific (and thus measurable) URL or claim code. At the site, offer them an array of additional learning tools, segmented by audience type, that they can access upon registration or newsletter sign-up.

The first rule in creating this additional content is to *know your audience*. It's not enough to take the content you already have and read it aloud or bind it differently; instead, consider the target audience for each type of content, and tailor your message from there.

For instance, it's generally understood that there are three different types of learners: visual, auditory, and kinesthetic. Visual learners benefit from video content, charts, graphs—anything that engages their eyes. Auditory learners do best with seminars, webinars, podcasts, and other predominantly spoken forms of communication. Kinesthetic learners need to interact with the content in an interactive, physical way—think science experiments, sports challenges, and role-playing activities. On an individual basis, it's impossible to know where your audience will fall.

However, when selling to a specific type of group, certain extensions of your existing content may make especially good sense. If possible, ask your sales prospect how the audience you will serve learns best—but make it known that you want everyone to benefit from your message and therefore can deliver the content in formats that appeal to all types of learners.

Presenting your customer with an array of content delivery formats designed to appeal to all segments of their team will help you seal the deal, especially if the content presents add-on value above and beyond your keynote or breakout session. Here are a few basic categories that these types of materials fall into.

Workbooks

A workbook can be a great supplement to content that involves a step-by-step approach to improvement or that instructs the reader or listener to perform a number of activities (typically in the genres of health and fitness, business, self-help, etc.). Authors of books like these can create workbooks in line with the content, incorporating any activities mentioned in the text and building from there to create a comprehensive resource for readers to use as they apply the concepts in the book.

By including a bonus workbook with every book purchase, you are offering readers an incentive to buy the book through your website, and you are giving them exclusive, value-added content.

If you instruct seminars or workshops, you can independently sell workbooks to attendees or include them within the cost of registration. Alternatively, you can post an abridged version of the workbook on your website or use the workbook as a reward to readers who signed up for your newsletter or RSS feed.

Audiobooks

Digital audio products are one of the most versatile content formats available. Like workbooks, your audio products can be sold alone or bundled to create new, high-value product sets exclusive to your website (a great way to compete with Amazon).

Back in the days of books on tape, audiobooks were dismissed as a minuscule category within publishing. Unless they were connected to the huge names in fiction, most audiobooks performed at a fraction of a percent of their paperback and hardcover equivalents in terms of units sold.

But as a generation became accustomed to always having earbuds shoved in their ears, and with the ease of acquiring digital audiobook content to listen to on electronic portable devices while driving, gardening, or just plain waiting somewhere, audiobooks are surging in popularity. According to the Audio Publishers Association, 2016 marked the third consecutive year with audiobook sales expansion of nearly 20 percent.[1]

If you have control of your audiobook rights, producing an audiobook can be fairly straightforward. (If your publisher holds those rights, they will either produce the audiobook on your behalf or sell those rights to a separate audiobook publisher.) Whether the idea of narrating it yourself horrifies or tempts you, I'd strongly encourage you to enlist a professional voice actor to do a read of your book. There's an art to properly voicing an audiobook so that the listener is not turned off by the vocal quality or diction patterns. An audiobook production house can point you toward voice talent options, or refer to the Resources page on ideasinfluenceandincome.com.

Once you've selected voice talent and the audiobook files are recorded, a production house will edit and master them to commercial standards. Most audiobook sales to consumers are digital, so having the MP3 files may be sufficient. However, if you plan to bundle the audiobook as an offering on your website or to include it with speaking engagements, a physical product like a CD can be a nice addition to your product mix.

In terms of reaching the end listener, while a number of new audiobook streaming services are emerging, Audible.com (owned by Amazon) is currently the go-to audiobook retailer. Audible.com also offers

---

1   Porter Anderson, "Audio Publishers Association: Third Year of Strong US Audiobook Sales Growth," *Publishing Perspectives*, June 7, 2017, https://publishingperspectives.com/2017/06/audiobook-sales-growth-us-2016-report/.

an interface called ACX (Audiobook Creation Exchange) for the DIY among you. This interface allows you to source voice talent and production services and provides a self-service tool to upload and sell your audiobooks on Audible.com.

Author Q&As

Author Q&As, or question and answer sections, are typically included in the backs of books. All you need to do to create a Q&A is prepare a list of questions and answers that are relevant to your content and audience. By sharing personal details and revealing the creative process behind the development of your ideas, you encourage a higher level of reader engagement. As a bonus, authors and speakers can leverage the Q&A as a part of a publicity campaign. Many publicists include a Q&A within online and print media kits to inform print, radio, and TV media contacts of potential angles for interview questions and human-interest stories.

The Q&A is also a great place to tease upcoming books or projects. Simply include a question about what you (as the author) might currently be working on. If a reader is interested enough in the book to read the author Q&A, they will likely look for a next book from you. Planting a seed of interest for your next book in the Q&A section is a good way to get those readers excited about your next project and helps build your audience base for the next book.

Self-assessments

Self-assessments are a great tool for engaging an audience and establishing yourself as a subject matter expert. These assessments can be presented as part of a book but are typically more effective online, and you can use them to capture customer data, evolving trends, or industry opinions. Self-assessments may take the form of a quiz or survey, and you can embed charts, graphs, and real-time survey results into your website to give fans statistics about the data they've provided.

How do you incentivize readers to complete the self-assessment? Consider holding a book giveaway on Twitter or Facebook where each completed assessment counts as a contest entry.

Training guides

A training guide is typically a separate publication that is paired with content designed to inform (rather than entertain). It should offer a week-by-week or half-day seminar approach to implementing the content, and it can be intended for individuals or organizations. Training guides usually include concept summaries, points to consider when implementing the concepts, and activities for groups and individuals.

Training guides can be used in several ways: as the foundation for the author or speaker's own training or coaching program, as one component of a training package, as a bonus readers receive when they buy the book, or as an add-on to be sold for additional revenue.

Book summaries

As the name implies, book summaries provide a short overview of a book and its key takeaways for readers who don't have the time or inclination to read the entire manuscript. And there are plenty of "unofficial" book summaries out there.

From time to time, our Greenleaf Book Group authors would bring to our attention a summary of their book listed for sale on Amazon. These summaries would have a cover that looked nothing like ours, be listed by a company name that is not ours, and contain content that the author never approved. On further research, we realized that these book summaries were not just the public domain classics marketed at disinterested teenage English students. There is a whole cottage industry of "follow-on" publishers watchfully studying nonfiction titles that sell well and then quickly producing what reads as a review of the work, touching the main points and themes without directly quoting too much of the actual content.

Understandably, this rubbed our authors the wrong way. These companies never acquired a license to produce the summaries—there is no mutual participation in a project like this. It's also rarely clear to the buyer that the summary is not "official" and connected to the actual full-length book, which could mean there's some questionable content for sale related to the author's book that is not author approved.

Facing this development, we took a quick pivot and decided to start producing our own summaries first, labeling them as *The Official Summary of [Book]*, for a few different reasons.

One, our authors make a living by repurposing and stretching every possible product out of their content, so not producing our own version costs our author an opportunity that some third party is grabbing. We needed to plant a flag with the official version right out of the gate to defend against the parties who might try to impose with their own version.

Two, given the tremendous effort that goes into building an author platform and its affiliated trust, it's too risky to have an unauthorized product put in front of our readers in case the summary is not well produced.

Three, after creating a few of these in a pilot program, we realized that while they didn't sell in great volume, they did have some other valuable uses. As a prospecting tool, a summary-length pamphlet to hand out and leave with a customer might give them just enough material to review and think on to keep you top of mind for a longer time, especially in a situation like a conference where you think giving everyone a full book might be a bit of overkill.

Content chunking and social media

Pulling nuggets of useful content from your book or presentation can be an easy way to create material for blogs and social media. Blog posts are an excellent marketing channel for sharing a top-ten list, how-to steps, a high-level exploration of a concept, or tips and recommendations for common problems.

Another option to consider is repurposing chunks of content into how-to PowerPoint presentations. After the content is created, you can then upload the presentations to SlideShare.net, the world's largest community for sharing presentations. Thought leaders who redistribute bite-sized pieces of material over the Internet—whether through blogs, video-sharing sites, or PowerPoint presentations—build brand awareness and instantly boost their visibility online.

Clearly, there are many ways to repurpose material into new revenue streams and lead-generation tools. When determining where to start, consider the type of content you already have and which new formats you can most easily apply it to. Going forward, evaluate the type of ancillary materials your audience would value most. If they're not already telling you, ask them! Your audience—and your bank account—will thank you in the end.

BUNDLE PRODUCT TO BOOST YOUR WEBSITE SALES

Amazon sells a boatload of books and a shipload of other stuff. In their quest to become your go-to shopping resource, they offer a huge range of products and often discount them steeply to get your shopping cart started . . . and books in particular seem to frequently become loss leaders. This sometimes alarms authors just entering the world of retail book distribution, who suddenly realize that the customer who once bought on the author's website can now buy the same book faster and cheaper on Amazon.

The discount Amazon places on titles usually comes out of Amazon's cut and does not affect what an author is paid through a publisher, but it can impact how effectively that author can sell product on their own website. It's important to remember, however, that there are at least two types of buyers—those who will just buy the book and those who are looking for a deeper experience. The buyer who just wants the book will probably not buy it from your author website if it is also available on Amazon. It is definitely difficult to compete with Amazon (or BN.com, Barnes & Noble's online store) for this customer—one-click purchasing, free shipping, and familiarity stack the cards in favor of the online retailers. However, the buyer seeking a more immersive experience is another story.

Some authors eschew Amazon, trying to keep a product monopoly limited to their website. This is a mistake—you'll never be able to attract the volume of users or offer the ease of purchase that Amazon does. As the saying goes, it's better to have 10 percent of the gold than 100 percent of the shaft.

That's not to say you shouldn't sell product on your website—in fact, you should use your website to sell product that offers a deeper experience for the fully immersive–type reader. Consider some of the formats described in this chapter as side products to sell with your book. Bundle the book with an audio supplement. Offer a self-assessment or workbook to accompany the book. Consider offering coaching or, better yet, a community where your readers can collaborate and support one another. Use access to assets like podcasts, sample chapters, and exclusive supplementary content as an incentive for newsletter sign-ups. And by all means, put a mention of these available website features at the back of your book.

One of Greenleaf Book Group's *New York Times* best-selling authors, Shirzad Chamine, does a wonderful job of this in the back of his book, *Positive Intelligence*. He provides website resources, a list of webinar and seminar topics he can address, and information about him as a keynote speaker. For the reader who wants to go deeper and bring the wisdom of the book into an organization, these tools provide the perfect bridge to move that forward.

You can also create "kits" of your content that are designed for bulk sales. For instance, your kit may include the print book, a code for the audio download, a DVD of you speaking on the topic, the book summary, and any proprietary charts or program flows you've created to support what you're teaching. Package it up impressively and you've got a comprehensive program on your hands—one that you can probably give a decent price tag.

Ultimately, the goal is to capture and stay in front of your reader in a way that enhances their connection with you (read: no spam!) and builds allegiance. Successfully doing so will help you compete not just with Amazon but also with every other author vying for attention (a far more formidable opponent). Another popular way to create revenue from your material is by using your own voice, quite literally.

USE SPEAKING AS AN INCOME GENERATOR

In the *Influence* section, we touched on professional speaking as a way to share your message and connect with an audience. Speaking can also be lucrative, both in terms of fees and the product sold to complement your presentation. Adam Robinson, author of *The Best Team Wins*, published his book on hiring in early 2017. According to Adam, "Our largest prospect organizations are now inviting us to speak to them, instead of us asking them if we can speak. That wouldn't have happened without *The Best Team Wins*." Adam's investment in thought leadership paid off.

Products serve a few specific needs for speakers. They reinforce your messaging and branding if packaged well and with consistency. They underscore your credibility and can differentiate you from your competitors. They can bring visibility, which can bring in speaking requests. And most importantly, they create value for your customers.

A company hiring a speaker to address leadership, employee engagement, customer service, or any other niche will want to know that there's some lasting impact from the fee paid to the speaker. The perception that a speaker is flying in, making a presentation that will be forgotten a week later, and flying out can be mitigated if the speaker offers product that helps to reinforce and maintain what was taught while they were in front of the group.

That doesn't mean you should just create product for the sake of creating product (in any scenario, really). Your product should be designed to add value as a resource to your audience. The long-form nature of a book makes it an obvious tool in the product category as it gives the audience a way to take a deeper dive into your content and reconnect with it at any time.

As the ancillary materials portion of this chapter discusses, your book may serve as the foundational piece from which these other products are derived. In other cases, especially if you need to address a specific topic that doesn't fit neatly into your book, a new standalone product is in order. For instance, if you speak on change management, you may have a separate product that deals specifically and more deeply with integrating teams after a merger.

Outside of your book, additional product formats you might consider to supplement your speaking engagement include—

- Audio programs with follow-up modules
- Workbooks
- Online learning modules
- Webinars
- A mobile app, if it provides regular content or a guided program
- Access to a membership site or community forum
- Merchandise like flashcards

You get the idea—there's no shortage of ideas around product. They all take time and money to develop, so be strategic about where they fit into your overall value proposition so your resources are used wisely.

OFFER ONLINE LEARNING PROGRAMS

Online learning programs are another excellent way to leverage content to build brand awareness, loyalty, and revenue. Some authors license their online learning programs to sites with established audiences, like Udemy and Lynda. Other authors choose to use a white label production service to develop online training modules that they can directly resell via their own website as part of a corporate training program. Author Shep Hyken (*The Amazement Revolution*), an expert in customer service, does an excellent job of showcasing his virtual interactive training program as a product through his website, hyken.com.

Online learning requires a different, more active content strategy than straight written material like books or case studies, but you can still use that material to create the foundation for your learning course.

Look for the high-level tools that you deliver to your reader (for example, a five-step process to engage employees) and consider working with an instructional designer to fill out the material necessary to teach your framework in the online learning format.

Don't try to force all of your existing content into this format without considering what makes a valuable online learning experience (i.e., don't stand in front of a camera and dictate your book, or your program will be panned for lack of effectiveness).

Use your content as a framework, then keep the following four points in mind as you build it into a powerful new product.

Storytelling brings meaning

Effective teaching involves modeling, whether that is through role-playing, case studies, group activities, or another format. Reading and rote memorization are not enough to create an active learning experience in an online format.

Storytelling makes up the backbone of these modeling exercises. Use relatable characters facing a conflict in a realistic scenario. This could be as simple as a role-play scene between an employee and manager discussing lack of engagement on the job.

Show how the application of your solution resolves the first level of the conflict, and then reiterate that learning moment to help drive home the takeaway. Of course, you'll create separate role-play scenarios for each level of conflict resolution. With our employee engagement example, it would start with trying to understand the employee's feelings and motivations and then move on to coach actions and behaviors.

Assignments and tasks bring applied learning

Active learning also occurs within assignments or tasks. A component of your online learning module might involve having the reader write, or participate in an online group discussion, about how they have dealt or would deal with a scenario described in your content. Their performance in this exercise would be assessed in part on how they used your solution model to address the problem at hand. This assessment can be done by you or by their course peers.

Community offers support

Teachers tend to teach in a single way, but students learn in many different ways. Building a community element into your online learning program will ensure that your students are supported for success emotionally and academically. This can be as simple as a closed Facebook group for your students or a separate tool within your online content delivery platform.

Study groups provide an opportunity for peers to collaborate and bounce ideas off of each other, or ask for help and clarification of concepts, in a safe environment. Quite often, a fellow student can offer a different explanation or past experience to clarify a concept that might bring a light bulb moment for another learner.

Provide outside resources to add value

When necessary, augment your instruction with additional outside resources to fill in or add to the content you're delivering.

Going back to our employee engagement example, if you're addressing the fact that part of engagement is making the right hire in the first place, consider providing resources around effective hiring practices. This doesn't take away from your authority but rather demonstrates your commitment to delivering a high-value product.

Outside resources can take the shape of additional reading recommendations, guest speakers, workshops, videos, and so on. Remember that your students have varied preferences for learning new material, so try to provide a mix of formats for them to take in this additional learning.

If you're working within your own content delivery platform, you have the freedom to design your course as you see fit—but you'll need to bring the audience. However, if you intend to use a third-party platform with an existing user base (like Udemy, Coursera, or Lynda), take a look at their typical courses and any listed course requirements and engineer your program per those guidelines.

As with any content strategy, understanding your user's preferences and goals on the front end will help to ensure a successful product launch and the resulting growth in brand awareness and revenue.

LICENSE YOUR ASSETS

Another way you can generate revenue through your ideas is through licensing, which involves giving permission to use your name, brand, or content to a third party to sell a product or service. Licensing can be a very effective way to expand your revenue channels and open doors to new audiences that you wouldn't have access to alone.

Licensing can take many forms. It requires your brand or content to be strong enough for another party to want to hitch their wagon to your star, so to speak. Licensing deals are made around a fit that brings value to the other party's audience.

Corporate licensing

Licensing to corporate clients is an opportunity that many nonfiction authors get very excited about. Financial planning guru David Bach, author of *The Automatic Millionaire* and *Start Late, Finish Rich*, has licensed his financial education content to some of the largest companies in the world.[2] The idea makes sense on the surface—you have quality, relevant content that could help a company to train or engage their employees, or they could even offer it as a premium to their own customers.

While I have seen this done successfully, it generally only happens if the author is willing to customize some aspect of the content to make it more exclusive to the company or if they bundle the book content along with another format, like webinars, in-person workshops, or a video series. There's no reason for a company to license the content otherwise—the whole book is already published and for sale, so there's no added value or access to negotiate. Some companies also aren't set up to manage payments from licensing deals structured on a royalty model, so reconciling and pursuing the revenue from these deals can become a challenge. A lump sum fee upfront may save you some headache in the long run.

Authors who also offer consulting, speaking gigs, or workshops will

---

2   Dan Schawbel, "David Bach on How to Build a Career without Going Broke," *Forbes,* January 16, 2012, https://www.forbes.com/sites/danschawbel/2012/01/16/david-bach-on-how-to-build-a-career-without-going-broke/#6517f791195c.

sometimes roll a customized book for each audience member into their overall speaking fee. This is a nice way to add value and a lasting reference tool (the book) to round out your speaking proposals.

Creating a custom edition for a company can be as simple as revising the cover to incorporate the company's name and logo and adding a brief foreword explaining why the company is bringing this content to its customers. That foreword is best written by someone at the company in order to strengthen their connection to the book.

For example, a bank might agree to license a custom version of a book on managing money to give to all customers who open a new savings account. The bank's name would be worked into the cover, and the bank's CEO might write a foreword or letter to the reader explaining the importance of reading this book to understand the basics of sound financial planning. As another example, life insurance expert Tony Steuer worked alongside a financial literacy education provider to create a co-branded combined version of his life insurance and disability workbooks, which was licensed to a major life insurance company for use in training.

Print-on-demand technology makes these custom editions easy to manage on quick timelines, even in smaller quantities. Even if the retail version of your book has been published with a traditional offset print run, you can simultaneously arrange these custom works by using print-on-demand partners like CreateSpace for printing services (not publishing).

While licensing doesn't have to be limited to custom editions of books, that is the most common and straightforward deal to make in this category. Beyond that, a strong brand can bring other product-licensing opportunities, like stuffed animals for children's book characters or board games and other themed merchandise for the huge breakout books that turn into summer blockbusters. These are typically reserved for hugely successful fiction works like *Harry Potter*, as you might imagine.

Pursuing licensing deals assumes you have the rights to license and print your book on your own. This may or may not be the case, depending on how you chose to bring your book to market.

If you have self-published, you should be free and clear to proceed. Hybrid authors usually have this flexibility, but since hybrid terms vary from publisher to publisher, it's best to confirm these rights. In traditional publishing deals, you generally cannot do this without your publisher's involvement unless you have carved out these rights on the front end, though here too, publishing agreements can vary from author to author.

Train the trainer

Many authors successfully launch speaking careers around delivering their own proprietary frameworks, methodologies, and so on. As I've said, this can be a lucrative way to monetize your content, but since there's only one you to deliver your message, it's not very scalable as a business strategy, and you may eventually burn out from travel exhaustion.

Here's another way that building a strong brand around your idea can help increase revenue: Once you do so, you can consider a train-the-trainer model to more or less franchise your speaking business.

Best-selling authors like Marcus Buckingham (*StrengthsFinder*), Melissa Hartwig (*The Whole 30*), and Jack Canfield (*Chicken Soup for the Soul* and *Success Principles*) use a train-the-trainer model to license their content to certify other qualified trainers in delivering their ideas. In most cases, this model works like a franchise system with the franchisee piggybacking on a successful brand and covering an assigned region.

This approach can be used online and offline. The online scenario is more common in direct-to-consumer programs, and your trainer (licensee) is often called a *coach* who provides a deeper level of guidance and support. Robert Kiyosaki's Rich Dad Coaching (based on his *Rich Dad, Poor Dad* series) is an example of this.

The offline version involves trainers or facilitators who deliver your content in person, usually to a corporate audience in the form of onsite workshops with some phone or email follow-up afterward.

In most cases, this model involves a revenue share between the licensor and licensee, and the licensee must follow established guidelines around the content delivery.

In other cases, the trainee is simply becoming certified in the trainer's system and is granted permission to use the brand but has to develop their own business opportunities from there. In the latter scenario, expect a trainee to pay a one-time fee to become certified (and possibly an annual certification renewal fee) but little to no revenue share from the business they develop since they don't enjoy the benefit of exclusive assigned territories or markets.

In both models, the rights to the intellectual property itself should remain with you, the licensor. Your licensees are simply authorized to deliver your content and leverage your brand. A strong noncompete and confidentiality agreement to protect your content and brand should be a part of your plan to roll out any coaching or training program involving outside representatives.

Licensing content for executive book summaries

There are a number of book summary services, primarily for business titles, that can handle the work of creating a book summary for you and bring the added benefit of wide visibility with a C-Suite audience. (GetAbstract, Soundview, and Success are a few of the more popular ones.)

Most of these summaries work on a non-exclusive basis, meaning you are not precluded from pursuing partnerships with them in addition to handling your own summary for retail sale, as described earlier in the chapter.

While some summary services will pay a small licensing fee in exchange for the license to create and distribute a summary, most do not (unless you are a very well-known author, of course). Even so, they are still worth pursuing because of the exposure they can bring. Most summary services have content-sharing deals with corporate and media partners. On the corporate side, the summary service may provide access to its content as a perk for employees (or members of an association), extending the reach of your message. On the media side, the summary service may have deals with online and print publications looking for additional content for their readers to bring more weight to features like top-ten lists.

Finally, a summary that performs well in English may be translated into other languages or into audio format, placing your name and idea in front of new markets and helping to boost your brand and platform.

MEMBERSHIP SITES

The appeal of developing a membership site is sort of like the appeal of running a software-as-a-service business; you develop the digital product once and then sell it repeatedly without adding additional overhead beyond administration and service support. In theory, it makes for a very profitable, scalable business. And for some, it is.

Why don't we see more authors with membership sites then? Because it is difficult to build the momentum to establish one with a healthy subscription list and then maintain the members through content that continually adds value they can't get anywhere else. Building and sustaining a membership site takes a strategic effort and the type of expert who is maniacally committed to their subject area, never tiring of continuing to develop expertise and insights to share.

Let's take a closer look at building a subscriber base and then building out content.

Subscriptions

If you've started the process of building out a newsletter database, you know that it can be a challenge to convince people to hand over an email address. A subscription makes a much bigger ask—hand over an email address and a bit of money every month, or possibly every year. You'll definitely need a rock-solid strategy and a passion for your message to build this subscriber base. This is where the power of a strong platform can again make all of the difference in terms of your content finding an audience.

As with any product launch, it will help to offer limited-time deep discounts on membership at the start, in the interest of establishing a base of initial users who, hopefully, will become raving fans and word-of-mouth promoters. When possible, capture their feedback to feature as an endorsement on the sales page of your site. Affirmations about your product from its users are always stronger than affirmations from you, its creator. (You're a little biased.) Retired Navy Seal and SEALFIT creator Mark Divine does a great job of highlighting user feedback and price tiers with his Unbeatable Mind Academy website.[3]

---

3 https://unbeatablemind.com/about-the-program/.

Some of the same promotional approaches used during the book launch can be repeated with your subscription site launch. Offering to provide sneak peek content for complementary sites with solid traffic can be a compelling, exclusive way for the partner site to offer value to their visitors while also helping to create visibility for your new product. The ideal partners are in the same space as you but don't directly compete. For example, a sports nutritionist might partner with a sports training site (cycling, bodybuilding, and so on) in this way.

Don't be shy about using your other products (books and any other content you've packaged) as a place to promote your membership site. If a reader has enjoyed your work, that's the best time to convince them to subscribe to a deeper level of content and access. Those who already know you and your work are well-qualified prospects.

High-value content

Well before you lock in your precious subscribers, you should be planning a matrix of premium content that your subscribers can't get elsewhere. Subscription site members are typically looking for a faster solution (more access to resources, help, and so on), a deeper understanding (a deeper dive into your area of expertise), or accountability (a support system to achieve a goal). Some membership sites give open access to everything as soon as a member signs up, and others feed (or open) these resources over time, especially if the subscriber is moving through a process or curriculum. Sales guru Jeffrey Gitomer's (*Little Red Book of Sales*) Gitomer Learning Academy is a good example of a subscription program with a curriculum program.

Some types of assets you might include are—

- In-depth articles that offer new insight or advice
- Live Q&A sessions with you or guest experts
- Exclusive webinars
- Educational video series
- Live lectures

- New tools or frameworks to help users implement your ideas
- Access to mastermind groups
- Forums that connect other community members

Your website analytics will provide valuable information about which resources are being used the most, giving you some guidance for developing future content assets. A monthly newsletter is a good way to keep your brand top of mind and offers a way for you to announce new features and resources, which you'll need to consistently add unless your subscription program is structured with an end point (one in which subscribers complete an education module and test out successfully, for example).

Some of the most successful membership sites put a heavy focus on building a connected community. For instance, youpreneur.com is a membership site offering education and support for aspiring entrepreneurs. They place a heavy emphasis on community forums, mastermind calls, and even tickets to in-person live events. When people feel like they are part of a larger movement and can directly relate to others working through a similar process or challenge, they feel supported and become more strongly committed to what they signed up for in the first place. They also motivate and even teach each other.

If a membership site makes sense for you, don't worry too much about the technical side. A quick Google search of *membership site software* will give you plenty of turnkey options to explore, including plugins that work in conjunction with existing WordPress sites (a popular website-building and hosting platform). The real work will come in hustling sign-ups and then delivering a steady stream of premium content or access.

SEEK OUT SPONSORS OR PARTNERSHIPS

Partnerships with outside companies or organizations are one of the most effective ways to extend the reach and impact of your message. Strong strategic partnerships allow you to connect with a platform that has already been built and a "tribe" that is ready for your message.

Partnerships can take time to build, but the payoff of exponentially increasing your ability to connect with new people makes them worthwhile to pursue.

For example, I worked with one author, Lorie Marrero, who is an expert in organization. Lorie's book *The Clutter Diet* helps people organize their homes. Lorie secured a partnership with Rubbermaid (they produce storage containers) and became a spokesperson for Goodwill (where you would likely donate items purged from your home during your decluttering effort). These partnerships gave Lorie a big credibility boost and helped to put her in front of consumers who were already looking for solutions she provides.

How do you build and maintain these strategic partnerships? Here are four tips to get started.

Help them help you

Just as in any relationship, if only one side is positioned to win, your partnership won't progress very far. A solid partnership has mutual benefit.

Think about the pitch you're making to the partner from their perspective. What is the win for them? Perhaps your partnership brings them a new service to offer their customers or a referral fee bonus or the opportunity to market to your list. Start with what's in it for them and make it irresistible.

Prioritize

Narrowing down partnership opportunities to find the ones with the most potential impact can be a daunting task. Begin by identifying the partners who serve the same core buyer as you.

As a simple example, an expert in the area of mergers and acquisitions might partner with an expert in change management. The two subjects go hand in hand but don't compete with each other. The same is true for experts in categories like exercise and weight loss where specialists are highly credentialed and tend to have deep knowledge in one area or program, like a certified trainer partnering with a registered dietitian. Sometimes the connection between services isn't as obvious, but the common fit with the audience is clear, such as a yoga studio partnering with a juice bar to cross promote.

Nurture the relationship and don't compete

Unlike the "close the deal or close the file" world of sales, developing business through strategic partnerships is heavy on long-term relationship building. These partnerships can take some time to get moving, so setting that expectation on the front end while developing a strong personal connection is important to mitigate disappointment or impatience during the ramp-up period.

Also consider the importance of not competing with your strategic partner in cases where your business offerings do overlap. It's best to develop a process to flag clients who were referred by strategic partners so they can be managed appropriately. Taking business away from the person who sent you a prospect is a surefire way to quickly kill a partnership.

Avoid exclusivity and keep exit options open

When working through the terms of your partnership agreement, protect your ability to work with other partners and your ability to walk away if the relationship isn't working.

Some partners will see the benefit you bring to their customers and push for an exclusive deal to make the value proposition even sweeter on their side. That's a win for them but not for you. In most cases, it makes more sense to stand your ground and decline exclusivity.

Similarly, avoid locking in to a restrictive long-term agreement that limits your ability to exit should things go south. Time spent managing a dysfunctional partnership that you can't exit is time that you're not spending on growing your business.

Keeping the exit options open can also provide a little push for both sides to proactively work at making the partnership effective. If your partner knows you can walk away from the table with just a reasonable amount of notice, they will be motivated to do their part to bring you a win quickly. And you will do the same.

A business development team focused on strategic partnerships plants seeds that require some care and nurturing on the front end but that can bear fruit for years to come. Treat your partners with the mutual respect that you would bring to any healthy relationship to boost your lead generation efforts and your bottom line.

Be strategic with the products you offer your audience

Clearly, there are many paths you can explore when it comes to pro-ductizing your content and extending its reach to new audiences. Some of these options may make sense for you, and others may not. Highly specific, niche content may work well in a licensing situation but not a membership site. Mainstream content from an author with a respectable platform may fit neatly into partnership opportunities but not licensing. Revisit the pain point you are trying to address, who your reader is, and how they take in content to find the option that best aligns with your audience.

Pay a visit to some of the websites referenced in this section for a bit of inspiration around monetizing content beyond the book, and then get creative with your own strategy on this front. Be as strategic in launching these programs as you are with your book, zeroing in on opportunities that allow you to access a wider audience to build your platform. Whether you simply offer a discount code for sales via your website or decide to undertake a larger challenge like building a subscription site, all of these efforts to extend your content beyond the book can open up valuable industry relationships that will serve you well in the long term.

Chapter 13

TO PUBLISH OR NOT?

Quick decisions are unsafe decisions.
—Sophocles

WITH ALL THE KNOWLEDGE GAINED from reading this book, is a book the right option for you? Of course it is.

The benefits of writing a book are many. It plants a flag to establish you as a leader in your niche. It is a tool to build leads. And used right, it's an income generator—as long as you actively incorporate it into a larger strategy and brand.

It's the rare author who is rich from book sales alone. Sure, some authors are well off and sell hundreds of thousands of books, but here's the real reason those authors are making money: They're thinking beyond the book.

BEYOND THE BOOK

Given that a book is a twenty-dollar container for an author's idea, much of the money authors make doesn't come from the sale of the book itself but rather the opportunities the book brings the author.

A professionally produced book gives you nearly instant credibility and opens doors to other streams of income. For nonfiction authors, the book is an extension of your business or expertise and another tool in your business-marketing tool belt.

As a reminder, here are some ways your book benefits you beyond book sales.

Speaking

Speakers who are authors are seen as more legitimate in the speaking business. A speaker who has written a book on their speaking topic is understood to be a deep expert in that subject area.

Teaching

Whether they are invited or hustle these gigs on their own, authors often teach their subjects at workshops, conferences, universities, continuing education classes, online, and in other venues. Again, you can roll the cost of the book into the cost of the workshop or make it required course reading material to be purchased in advance.

Ancillary materials

The content in your book can be repurposed into teacher's guides, workbooks, online learning modules, and video education series, among other formats. If you have the rights, be creative and deliver your content in as many formats as possible so your audience can find just the product they need.

Resident expert or correspondent

A successful book can give you the credibility to serve as an expert or correspondent to media and organizations, which in turn can help to reinforce your brand value and visibility. While most media outlets won't pay you to appear on their programs, the exposure can be priceless.

You get the idea—the book lays the groundwork for additional initiatives. Yes, retail success is important to any author. But when determining the real return on investment of all of the time dumped into finishing and publishing your book, the key is to think beyond the book and look for ways you can leverage your new position as a published author to find ways to generate income, grow your platform, and identify new outlets for your message (and your book).

IS THIS THE RIGHT TIME TO WRITE A BOOK?

Writing a book is a daunting task for most and a long process to boot. On top of that, many would-be authors doubt whether their ideas are book-worthy. My hope is that you'll be able to use this book as a resource to help you move forward—but you may be questioning whether this hustle is worth it, given whatever else is going on in your life. How do you know when the time is right for you to write a book? Here are four key elements to look for.

Commitment

Writing a book requires an enormous amount of time and thought commitment, but if an author wants to see any degree of commercial success, it also requires a commitment to promote and hustle sales. It takes months, sometimes years, to write a book. Once it's complete, you're looking at another six to nine months for a national distribution rollout. (Digital publishing options obviously can shorten that timeframe but limit availability.) Having support on the production and writing side in addition to outside eyes to advise on brand matters will make the journey much more manageable for authors during the writing process and during the launch stage.

An author should be in a long-term mindset for the book project to succeed, which is also necessary to stay engaged around executing very deliberate content and marketing plans that create lasting value.

Differentiated approach

If you have a highly differentiated approach to business in general, customer service, health and wellness, product development, or whatever you specialize in, the book-writing process will go much more smoothly because the value proposition is already clear, and there is likely a lot of supporting material. The book launch itself will also be more successful since readers and the media are drawn to fresh ideas, in turn bringing attention and awareness back to your overall brand.

If you don't think you have such a differentiated approach, take a fresh look at the *Ideas* section of this book for some advice on how to narrow in on the distinctive aspects of your brand. Certainly, there is something that makes you and what you do different. It can be hard to see for yourself, by yourself. If you're stuck on this front, call in the help of a brand strategist so you can get clear on your competitive advantage.

Flexibility

Flexibility applies in a few different ways. First, writing a book is ideally a collaborative process, so the author should be open and coachable in terms of feedback and changes to make the final product as marketable as it can be. Second, it sometimes turns out that a book is not the right format for the author's content. Some ideas originally intended for book form are really more appropriate for magazine articles, short ebooks, or even blog posts. A carefully executed piece at any one of these shorter lengths is just as effective, and probably more shareable, than a full-length book, so there's no shame in keeping it succinct. Finally, a book-length manuscript typically contains pieces of content that can stand alone for promotional purposes (think excerpts, tweets, blog posts, etc.). The flexible author will be receptive to these uses and even proactive about identifying them in the manuscript, in the interest of getting the most impact from the work of writing.

Willingness to engage

I've been on the frontlines of the publishing business for over a decade and in the broader media business for almost twice that. When authors learn this and hear of our company's dozens of *New York Times* bestsellers, they ask me for the secret behind successful launches. While the bibliophile in me would love to say that a well-written book ultimately finds an audience, it's just not true in a climate of oversupply and under-demand (this is especially pronounced with books but really applies to all media).

Generally, the most successful books are those that are attached to an author who is committed to engaging his or her audience, building a community, and serving those people from a place of purpose. A book is a social product, and there's no overstating the need for ongoing participation by the author. That engagement is imperative to growing the reader relationships that drive word of mouth, positive reviews, strong brand connections, and retail book sales.

If an author isn't ready for that level of commitment, that doesn't mean that he or she shouldn't hunker down and write a book (or something shorter). Today's print-on-demand digital publishing options make it possible for books of all lengths to be published and available online in a fast and relatively inexpensive model. The multiple benefits of creating long-form content remain, and the pressure and risk around a traditional retail book launch are removed. That said, after reading this far, you've learned that a digital-only distribution model greatly limits brick-and-mortar distribution (and discovery), so the author's team would be wise to consult an expert to weigh the pros and cons of digital publishing versus a traditional or hybrid publishing model to determine the best approach for their project and goals.

Making the choice

Writing a book is not for the faint of heart, but neither is the process of building a brand and growing an audience. With the right author and support team in place, a book can serve as a foundational piece for the messaging, marketing, and publicity efforts needed to build awareness, value, and influence for the long term.

If your book adequately conveys the promise and purpose of your core business work, it can be a great tool to establish credibility and help attract prequalified prospects that want the additional benefit of your speaking, consulting, or coaching services. Some authors are content to use digital publishing and an online-only distribution approach, but if you're seeking wider distribution of physical copies in airport bookstores and so forth, you'll most likely need to partner with an established publisher or distributor.

A word of caution: Do your research! From self-publishing to traditional publishing and hybrid models in between, there are multiple ways to publish. The approach that is best for you will depend on your goals, timeline, genre, and resources. Just as in any other industry, quality can vary—so do your homework to avoid the less favorable publishing routes.

Conclusion

YOUR BOOK MATTERS

THE LANDSCAPE OF THOUGHT LEADERSHIP HAS CHANGED. Once a status reserved for academics, today's thought leaders have deep expertise on a specialty *and* strong, carefully developed personal brands. Today, your ideas can make a difference without being published in a groundbreaking, peer-reviewed research paper brought out in a professional journal.

Being a thought leader is no longer a conferred title bestowed by a handful of third parties, like media institutions and universities. Now, those third parties still factor into the authority mix, but your ability to directly connect with and influence your audience has changed dramatically. You have an audience waiting for the answers you provide. You need to devise a plan to impact and connect with them.

A writer's view of the value of their work can be distorted by the extensive work put into finishing it. The value of your book has nothing to do with the time it took you to complete it. The value has to do with your ability to impact an audience with the message in your book and the ecosystem built around it.

Writers who fall in love with their own work by virtue of the labor that went into it can fall into the "If I build it, they will come" trap. *That was hard work, so surely everyone will appreciate it and buy my book!* No, they won't—not without a plan to let them know why they should give you two weeks of attention to read your book. You must build the book *and* build the audience *and* build the business strategy that ties it all together. I've made the point many times in this book that writers can be sidelined by focusing completely on the idea without minding the influence and income, but it can also be the case that authors focus on influence or income at the expense of a solid idea. We're seeking balance between the three, as they all depend upon each other to succeed.

If you don't enjoy writing, seek help. Get a developmental editor or manuscript coach to help you crank out an outline, or revisit the *Ideas* section to learn more about hiring a ghostwriter. If you are an introvert who shudders at the idea of self-promotion, hire a publicist and a social media team to help you carry your personal brand forward. And if you lack confidence on the business side of things, there are plenty of consultants and resources available to help you get the most of your content in any of the formats described in the *Income* section. (Many of these are listed on the Resources page at ideasinfluenceandincome.com.)

As technology continues to interconnect us, our access to like-minded communities grows. That access brings powerful new connections and relationships, but it also introduces more competition for the mindshare of your target audience.

Whether you're studying the foundations of content marketing or the impact of social media, the power of story is a linchpin in effective marketing. The longer length of a book (relative to other content forms) gives the writer more room to weave stories into a narrative, to teach through examples, and to create memorable scenarios to help readers relate to their ideas. All of these tools help to make ideas "sticky" and, done well, give the reader a road map to take action.

START THE HUSTLE

Now that you have a game plan for developing and launching your book, your challenge will be to think about its success in the long term. Six weeks of promotion is not enough to sustain your thought-leadership push. That six weeks of promotion is important, of course, but it should be followed by additional initiatives or phases to keep momentum moving along.

For example, we covered alternative formats like workbooks in Chapter 12 of the *Income* section. Those can be created during the editorial process of the book itself, or you can tackle them afterward. It will probably depend on your energy level around writing more material, so ask for help if the thought of writing one more word makes your stomach turn.

If you have already launched your book and are wishing you had known some of this information sooner, all is not lost. Some authors move on to do completely new works, but depending on your situation, it may make sense to rerelease it in a different format (i.e., if you started with hardcover, come out with a paperback edition) or do a second edition with updated content.

In both of these cases, the new release will receive a fresh ISBN (product identifier) and will be seen by retailers as a new product. It's a bit like credit—your chances to get some attention from media or retailers are stronger with a new product with no sales history (no credit) than with an old product with a weak sales history (bad credit).

A new edition also gives you the opportunity to update the cover with any powerful reviews awards, or endorsements you may have received on your first edition. Consider reader feedback as well, especially around areas where they were confused or thought an idea needed to be better supported. A second edition is an excellent way to refine your book to make sure it is serving your reader as you intended.

With a launch at any stage or iteration, you have an opportunity to put the tactics in the *Influence* section to use again. Launches give people something to talk about and can help create the valuable brand impressions that keep you on the radar of the audience you worked so hard to build.

One of my favorite things about running a publishing company is hearing how my authors' books impact the lives of strangers. I'm sure I only hear a fraction of those stories, but when an author forwards an email to me from a reader they don't know who took the time to reach out and share how that book changed their life, it gives me goosebumps. That's how making a difference feels. That's how giving back feels. That's how building a book to be proud of feels.

Now, it's your turn. If you need me, reread all or part of this book, visit the ideasinfluenceandinccme.com website, or reach out to me directly. I'm here to support you, I'm grateful for your attention, and I can't wait until we have a champagne toast to celebrate your new book.

ACKNOWLEDGMENTS

THE PROCESS OF WRITING THIS BOOK was, predictably, a learning experience. I could not have done it without the passionate and amazingly talented team at Greenleaf Book Group, both past and present.

I knew that writing a book would give me a better understanding and appreciation of the writing process that so many of my authors are actively pushing through, and it did not fail in that regard. I have a new respect and now sympathy, rather than empathy, for what it feels like to work through that experience. The specific team assigned to the production phase of my book—Nathan True, Lindsey Clark, Brian Phillips, Neil Gonzalez, and Kirsten Andrews—you are gifted and patient experts at what you do, and I have a deep respect for your work. And of course, my book kind of sort of stayed on schedule with no thanks to me, but many thanks to the steadfast and devoted attention of Carrie Jones, our director of production, who wrangled me with her usual diplomacy and patience. Carrie, you are a saint and a treasure.

The team that takes over once the book has gone to press and guides the author through the challenging launch phase of the book is rarely recognized in the acknowledgments, simply due to the fact that the author generally has not worked with them at the time the acknowledgments are written. That's a shame because their work is critical and deserving of recognition! Corrin Foster, you're a rock star and a marketing goddess. Steve Elizalde, what bookstore buyer could say no to you? Thank you both for your efforts to bring my book forward into the world, in both physical and digital forms.

Then there are the people who ride shotgun with you during a project like this and step up to save the day when you're stuck. Emilie Lyons, thanks for being a steward for this book from start to finish, helping with all sorts of things to keep it moving forward. Your support and smarts made all the difference in refining and finishing this book. Claire Jentsch, you knock out every writing-related assignment with gusto and care. Sujan Trivedi and Bryan Goodwin, you both handled all of my questions about publishing law with humor and patience.

Last but far from least—Farm Boy, you make me a better person. Thank you for everything.

RESOURCES

Visit www.IdeasInfluenceandIncome.com

Looking for additional help and resources? Visit the *Ideas, Influence, and Income* website, and you'll find

Tools

I share my favorite resources for writing and launching your book.

White Papers

Get into the specifics of topics like how to write a nonfiction book proposal, authority-based marketing, and more.

Assessments

Use my online quiz to evaluate your platform and determine your individual Expert Score. You'll leave with tools and tips to boost your thought leader status.

Podcast Episodes

As the host of *Published*, a podcast all about book publishing, I interview experts on topics like working with a publicist, what retail buyers are looking for, and building an audience. Full episodes are also available on iTunes.

My Speaking Information

Browse the topics that I regularly speak on and find handouts from past speaking engagements.

Visit www.IdeasInfluenceandIncome.com

INDEX

ABOUT THE AUTHOR

TANYA HALL is the chief executive officer of Greenleaf Book Group, where she drives growth efforts and fosters a culture built on serving authors. Founded in 1997, Greenleaf represents over 1,200 active titles, with dozens of *New York Times* and *Wall Street Journal* bestsellers.

Prior to her current role, Tanya worked directly with Greenleaf's authors to develop publishing strategies; spearheaded growth strategies, including Greenleaf's ebook program and the River Grove digital-first imprint; and built Greenleaf's distribution organization, working directly with retailers and wholesalers to develop one of the fastest-growing distribution businesses in the industry. Before joining the publishing industry, Tanya worked in digital media and in television production for *Extra!* and E! Entertainment Television.

Learn more at

www.GreenleafBookGroup.com

www.IdeasInfluenceandIncome.com